I0329485

C-406 CAREER EXAMINATION SERIES

This is your PASSBOOK for...

Jail Guard

Test Preparation Study Guide
Questions & Answers

NLC®

NATIONAL LEARNING CORPORATION®

National Learning Corporation

212 Michael Drive, Syosset, NY 11791
(516) 921-8888 • www.passbooks.com
E-mail: info@passbooks.com

PASSBOOK® SERIES

THE *PASSBOOK® SERIES* has been created to prepare applicants and candidates for the ultimate academic battlefield – the examination room.

At some time in our lives, each and every one of us may be required to take an examination – for validation, matriculation, admission, qualification, registration, certification, or licensure.

Based on the assumption that every applicant or candidate has met the basic formal educational standards, has taken the required number of courses, and read the necessary texts, the *PASSBOOK® SERIES* furnishes the one special preparation which may assure passing with confidence, instead of failing with insecurity. Examination questions – together with answers – are furnished as the basic vehicle for study so that the mysteries of the examination and its compounding difficulties may be eliminated or diminished by a sure method.

This book is meant to help you pass your examination provided that you qualify and are serious in your objective.

The entire field is reviewed through the huge store of content information which is succinctly presented through a provocative and challenging approach – the question-and-answer method.

A climate of success is established by furnishing the correct answers at the end of each test.

You soon learn to recognize types of questions, forms of questions, and patterns of questioning. You may even begin to anticipate expected outcomes.

You perceive that many questions are repeated or adapted so that you can gain acute insights, which may enable you to score many sure points.

You learn how to confront new questions, or types of questions, and to attack them confidently and work out the correct answers.

You note objectives and emphases, and recognize pitfalls and dangers, so that you may make positive educational adjustments.

Moreover, you are kept fully informed in relation to new concepts, methods, practices, and directions in the field.

You discover that you are actually taking the examination all the time: you are preparing for the examination by "taking" an examination, not by reading extraneous and/or supererogatory textbooks.

In short, this PASSBOOK®, used directedly, should be an important factor in helping you to pass your test.

JAIL GUARD

DUTIES
Maintains security in a jail. In charge of prisoners awaiting trial or sentencing and those sentenced to jail terms, generally under one year. Performs related duties.

SCOPE OF THE WRITTEN TEST
The written test will be designed to test for knowledge, skills, and/or abilities in such areas as:

1. Principles and practices of jail operations and security;
2. Working with prisoners in a jail setting;
3. Understanding and interpreting written material;
4. Report writing;
5. Verbal ability; and
6. Arithmetic

HOW TO TAKE A TEST

I. YOU MUST PASS AN EXAMINATION

A. WHAT EVERY CANDIDATE SHOULD KNOW

Examination applicants often ask us for help in preparing for the written test. What can I study in advance? What kinds of questions will be asked? How will the test be given? How will the papers be graded?

As an applicant for a civil service examination, you may be wondering about some of these things. Our purpose here is to suggest effective methods of advance study and to describe civil service examinations.

Your chances for success on this examination can be increased if you know how to prepare. Those "pre-examination jitters" can be reduced if you know what to expect. You can even experience an adventure in good citizenship if you know why civil service exams are given.

B. WHY ARE CIVIL SERVICE EXAMINATIONS GIVEN?

Civil service examinations are important to you in two ways. As a citizen, you want public jobs filled by employees who know how to do their work. As a job seeker, you want a fair chance to compete for that job on an equal footing with other candidates. The best-known means of accomplishing this two-fold goal is the competitive examination.

Exams are widely publicized throughout the nation. They may be administered for jobs in federal, state, city, municipal, town or village governments or agencies.

Any citizen may apply, with some limitations, such as the age or residence of applicants. Your experience and education may be reviewed to see whether you meet the requirements for the particular examination. When these requirements exist, they are reasonable and applied consistently to all applicants. Thus, a competitive examination may cause you some uneasiness now, but it is your privilege and safeguard.

C. HOW ARE CIVIL SERVICE EXAMS DEVELOPED?

Examinations are carefully written by trained technicians who are specialists in the field known as "psychological measurement," in consultation with recognized authorities in the field of work that the test will cover. These experts recommend the subject matter areas or skills to be tested; only those knowledges or skills important to your success on the job are included. The most reliable books and source materials available are used as references. Together, the experts and technicians judge the difficulty level of the questions.

Test technicians know how to phrase questions so that the problem is clearly stated. Their ethics do not permit "trick" or "catch" questions. Questions may have been tried out on sample groups, or subjected to statistical analysis, to determine their usefulness.

Written tests are often used in combination with performance tests, ratings of training and experience, and oral interviews. All of these measures combine to form the best-known means of finding the right person for the right job.

II. HOW TO PASS THE WRITTEN TEST

A. NATURE OF THE EXAMINATION

To prepare intelligently for civil service examinations, you should know how they differ from school examinations you have taken. In school you were assigned certain definite pages to read or subjects to cover. The examination questions were quite detailed and usually emphasized memory. Civil service exams, on the other hand, try to discover your present ability to perform the duties of a position, plus your potentiality to learn these duties. In other words, a civil service exam attempts to predict how successful you will be. Questions cover such a broad area that they cannot be as minute and detailed as school exam questions.

In the public service similar kinds of work, or positions, are grouped together in one "class." This process is known as *position-classification.* All the positions in a class are paid according to the salary range for that class. One class title covers all of these positions, and they are all tested by the same examination.

B. FOUR BASIC STEPS

1) Study the announcement

How, then, can you know what subjects to study? Our best answer is: "Learn as much as possible about the class of positions for which you've applied." The exam will test the knowledge, skills and abilities needed to do the work.

Your most valuable source of information about the position you want is the official exam announcement. This announcement lists the training and experience qualifications. Check these standards and apply only if you come reasonably close to meeting them.

The brief description of the position in the examination announcement offers some clues to the subjects which will be tested. Think about the job itself. Review the duties in your mind. Can you perform them, or are there some in which you are rusty? Fill in the blank spots in your preparation.

Many jurisdictions preview the written test in the exam announcement by including a section called "Knowledge and Abilities Required," "Scope of the Examination," or some similar heading. Here you will find out specifically what fields will be tested.

2) Review your own background

Once you learn in general what the position is all about, and what you need to know to do the work, ask yourself which subjects you already know fairly well and which need improvement. You may wonder whether to concentrate on improving your strong areas or on building some background in your fields of weakness. When the announcement has specified "some knowledge" or "considerable knowledge," or has used adjectives like "beginning principles of..." or "advanced ... methods," you can get a clue as to the number and difficulty of questions to be asked in any given field. More questions, and hence broader coverage, would be included for those subjects which are more important in the work. Now weigh your strengths and weaknesses against the job requirements and prepare accordingly.

3) Determine the level of the position

Another way to tell how intensively you should prepare is to understand the level of the job for which you are applying. Is it the entering level? In other words, is this the position in which beginners in a field of work are hired? Or is it an intermediate or advanced level? Sometimes this is indicated by such words as "Junior" or "Senior" in the class title. Other jurisdictions use Roman numerals to designate the level – Clerk I, Clerk II, for example. The word "Supervisor" sometimes appears in the title. If the level is not indicated by the title, check the description of duties. Will you be working under very close supervision, or will you have responsibility for independent decisions in this work?

4) Choose appropriate study materials

Now that you know the subjects to be examined and the relative amount of each subject to be covered, you can choose suitable study materials. For beginning level jobs, or even advanced ones, if you have a pronounced weakness in some aspect of your training, read a modern, standard textbook in that field. Be sure it is up to date and has general coverage. Such books are normally available at your library, and the librarian will be glad to help you locate one. For entry-level positions, questions of appropriate difficulty are chosen – neither highly advanced questions, nor those too simple. Such questions require careful thought but not advanced training.

If the position for which you are applying is technical or advanced, you will read more advanced, specialized material. If you are already familiar with the basic principles of your field, elementary textbooks would waste your time. Concentrate on advanced textbooks and technical periodicals. Think through the concepts and review difficult problems in your field.

These are all general sources. You can get more ideas on your own initiative, following these leads. For example, training manuals and publications of the government agency which employs workers in your field can be useful, particularly for technical and professional positions. A letter or visit to the government department involved may result in more specific study suggestions, and certainly will provide you with a more definite idea of the exact nature of the position you are seeking.

III. KINDS OF TESTS

Tests are used for purposes other than measuring knowledge and ability to perform specified duties. For some positions, it is equally important to test ability to make adjustments to new situations or to profit from training. In others, basic mental abilities not dependent on information are essential. Questions which test these things may not appear as pertinent to the duties of the position as those which test for knowledge and information. Yet they are often highly important parts of a fair examination. For very general questions, it is almost impossible to help you direct your study efforts. What we can do is to point out some of the more common of these general abilities needed in public service positions and describe some typical questions.

1) General information

Broad, general information has been found useful for predicting job success in some kinds of work. This is tested in a variety of ways, from vocabulary lists to questions about current events. Basic background in some field of work, such as sociology or economics, may be sampled in a group of questions. Often these are principles which have become familiar to most persons through exposure rather than through formal training. It is difficult to advise you how to study for these questions; being alert to the world around you is our best suggestion.

2) Verbal ability

An example of an ability needed in many positions is verbal or language ability. Verbal ability is, in brief, the ability to use and understand words. Vocabulary and grammar tests are typical measures of this ability. Reading comprehension or paragraph interpretation questions are common in many kinds of civil service tests. You are given a paragraph of written material and asked to find its central meaning.

3) Numerical ability

Number skills can be tested by the familiar arithmetic problem, by checking paired lists of numbers to see which are alike and which are different, or by interpreting charts and graphs. In the latter test, a graph may be printed in the test booklet which you are asked to use as the basis for answering questions.

4) Observation

A popular test for law-enforcement positions is the observation test. A picture is shown to you for several minutes, then taken away. Questions about the picture test your ability to observe both details and larger elements.

5) Following directions

In many positions in the public service, the employee must be able to carry out written instructions dependably and accurately. You may be given a chart with several columns, each column listing a variety of information. The questions require you to carry out directions involving the information given in the chart.

6) Skills and aptitudes

Performance tests effectively measure some manual skills and aptitudes. When the skill is one in which you are trained, such as typing or shorthand, you can practice. These tests are often very much like those given in business school or high school courses. For many of the other skills and aptitudes, however, no short-time preparation can be made. Skills and abilities natural to you or that you have developed throughout your lifetime are being tested.

Many of the general questions just described provide all the data needed to answer the questions and ask you to use your reasoning ability to find the answers. Your best preparation for these tests, as well as for tests of facts and ideas, is to be at your physical and mental best. You, no doubt, have your own methods of getting into an exam-taking mood and keeping "in shape." The next section lists some ideas on this subject.

IV. KINDS OF QUESTIONS

Only rarely is the "essay" question, which you answer in narrative form, used in civil service tests. Civil service tests are usually of the short-answer type. Full instructions for answering these questions will be given to you at the examination. But in case this is your first experience with short-answer questions and separate answer sheets, here is what you need to know:

1) Multiple-choice Questions

Most popular of the short-answer questions is the "multiple choice" or "best answer" question. It can be used, for example, to test for factual knowledge, ability to solve problems or judgment in meeting situations found at work.

A multiple-choice question is normally one of three types—

- It can begin with an incomplete statement followed by several possible endings. You are to find the one ending which *best* completes the statement, although some of the others may not be entirely wrong.
- It can also be a complete statement in the form of a question which is answered by choosing one of the statements listed.

- It can be in the form of a problem – again you select the best answer.

Here is an example of a multiple-choice question with a discussion which should give you some clues as to the method for choosing the right answer:

When an employee has a complaint about his assignment, the action which will *best* help him overcome his difficulty is to

A. discuss his difficulty with his coworkers
B. take the problem to the head of the organization
C. take the problem to the person who gave him the assignment
D. say nothing to anyone about his complaint

In answering this question, you should study each of the choices to find which is best. Consider choice "A" – Certainly an employee may discuss his complaint with fellow employees, but no change or improvement can result, and the complaint remains unresolved. Choice "B" is a poor choice since the head of the organization probably does not know what assignment you have been given, and taking your problem to him is known as "going over the head" of the supervisor. The supervisor, or person who made the assignment, is the person who can clarify it or correct any injustice. Choice "C" is, therefore, correct. To say nothing, as in choice "D," is unwise. Supervisors have and interest in knowing the problems employees are facing, and the employee is seeking a solution to his problem.

2) True/False Questions

The "true/false" or "right/wrong" form of question is sometimes used. Here a complete statement is given. Your job is to decide whether the statement is right or wrong.

SAMPLE: A roaming cell-phone call to a nearby city costs less than a non-roaming call to a distant city.

This statement is wrong, or false, since roaming calls are more expensive.

This is not a complete list of all possible question forms, although most of the others are variations of these common types. You will always get complete directions for answering questions. Be sure you understand *how* to mark your answers – ask questions until you do.

V. RECORDING YOUR ANSWERS

Computer terminals are used more and more today for many different kinds of exams.

For an examination with very few applicants, you may be told to record your answers in the test booklet itself. Separate answer sheets are much more common. If this separate answer sheet is to be scored by machine – and this is often the case – it is highly important that you mark your answers correctly in order to get credit.

An electronic scoring machine is often used in civil service offices because of the speed with which papers can be scored. Machine-scored answer sheets must be marked with a pencil, which will be given to you. This pencil has a high graphite content which responds to the electronic scoring machine. As a matter of fact, stray dots may register as answers, so do not let your pencil rest on the answer sheet while you are pondering the correct answer. Also, if your pencil lead breaks or is otherwise defective, ask for another.

Since the answer sheet will be dropped in a slot in the scoring machine, be careful not to bend the corners or get the paper crumpled.

The answer sheet normally has five vertical columns of numbers, with 30 numbers to a column. These numbers correspond to the question numbers in your test booklet. After each number, going across the page are four or five pairs of dotted lines. These short dotted lines have small letters or numbers above them. The first two pairs may also have a "T" or "F" above the letters. This indicates that the first two pairs only are to be used if the questions are of the true-false type. If the questions are multiple choice, disregard the "T" and "F" and pay attention only to the small letters or numbers.

Answer your questions in the manner of the sample that follows:

32. The largest city in the United States is
    A. Washington, D.C.
    B. New York City
    C. Chicago
    D. Detroit
    E. San Francisco

1) Choose the answer you think is best. (New York City is the largest, so "B" is correct.)
2) Find the row of dotted lines numbered the same as the question you are answering. (Find row number 32)
3) Find the pair of dotted lines corresponding to the answer. (Find the pair of lines under the mark "B.")
4) Make a solid black mark between the dotted lines.

VI. BEFORE THE TEST

Common sense will help you find procedures to follow to get ready for an examination. Too many of us, however, overlook these sensible measures. Indeed, nervousness and fatigue have been found to be the most serious reasons why applicants fail to do their best on civil service tests. Here is a list of reminders:

- Begin your preparation early – Don't wait until the last minute to go scurrying around for books and materials or to find out what the position is all about.
- Prepare continuously – An hour a night for a week is better than an all-night cram session. This has been definitely established. What is more, a night a week for a month will return better dividends than crowding your study into a shorter period of time.
- Locate the place of the exam – You have been sent a notice telling you when and where to report for the examination. If the location is in a different town or otherwise unfamiliar to you, it would be well to inquire the best route and learn something about the building.
- Relax the night before the test – Allow your mind to rest. Do not study at all that night. Plan some mild recreation or diversion; then go to bed early and get a good night's sleep.
- Get up early enough to make a leisurely trip to the place for the test – This way unforeseen events, traffic snarls, unfamiliar buildings, etc. will not upset you.
- Dress comfortably – A written test is not a fashion show. You will be known by number and not by name, so wear something comfortable.

- Leave excess paraphernalia at home – Shopping bags and odd bundles will get in your way. You need bring only the items mentioned in the official notice you received; usually everything you need is provided. Do not bring reference books to the exam. They will only confuse those last minutes and be taken away from you when in the test room.
- Arrive somewhat ahead of time – If because of transportation schedules you must get there very early, bring a newspaper or magazine to take your mind off yourself while waiting.
- Locate the examination room – When you have found the proper room, you will be directed to the seat or part of the room where you will sit. Sometimes you are given a sheet of instructions to read while you are waiting. Do not fill out any forms until you are told to do so; just read them and be prepared.
- Relax and prepare to listen to the instructions
- If you have any physical problem that may keep you from doing your best, be sure to tell the test administrator. If you are sick or in poor health, you really cannot do your best on the exam. You can come back and take the test some other time.

VII. AT THE TEST

The day of the test is here and you have the test booklet in your hand. The temptation to get going is very strong. Caution! There is more to success than knowing the right answers. You must know how to identify your papers and understand variations in the type of short-answer question used in this particular examination. Follow these suggestions for maximum results from your efforts:

1) Cooperate with the monitor

The test administrator has a duty to create a situation in which you can be as much at ease as possible. He will give instructions, tell you when to begin, check to see that you are marking your answer sheet correctly, and so on. He is not there to guard you, although he will see that your competitors do not take unfair advantage. He wants to help you do your best.

2) Listen to all instructions

Don't jump the gun! Wait until you understand all directions. In most civil service tests you get more time than you need to answer the questions. So don't be in a hurry. Read each word of instructions until you clearly understand the meaning. Study the examples, listen to all announcements and follow directions. Ask questions if you do not understand what to do.

3) Identify your papers

Civil service exams are usually identified by number only. You will be assigned a number; you must not put your name on your test papers. Be sure to copy your number correctly. Since more than one exam may be given, copy your exact examination title.

4) Plan your time

Unless you are told that a test is a "speed" or "rate of work" test, speed itself is usually not important. Time enough to answer all the questions will be provided, but this does not mean that you have all day. An overall time limit has been set. Divide the total time (in minutes) by the number of questions to determine the approximate time you have for each question.

5) Do not linger over difficult questions

If you come across a difficult question, mark it with a paper clip (useful to have along) and come back to it when you have been through the booklet. One caution if you do this – be sure to skip a number on your answer sheet as well. Check often to be sure that you have not lost your place and that you are marking in the row numbered the same as the question you are answering.

6) Read the questions

Be sure you know what the question asks! Many capable people are unsuccessful because they failed to *read* the questions correctly.

7) Answer all questions

Unless you have been instructed that a penalty will be deducted for incorrect answers, it is better to guess than to omit a question.

8) Speed tests

It is often better NOT to guess on speed tests. It has been found that on timed tests people are tempted to spend the last few seconds before time is called in marking answers at random – without even reading them – in the hope of picking up a few extra points. To discourage this practice, the instructions may warn you that your score will be "corrected" for guessing. That is, a penalty will be applied. The incorrect answers will be deducted from the correct ones, or some other penalty formula will be used.

9) Review your answers

If you finish before time is called, go back to the questions you guessed or omitted to give them further thought. Review other answers if you have time.

10) Return your test materials

If you are ready to leave before others have finished or time is called, take ALL your materials to the monitor and leave quietly. Never take any test material with you. The monitor can discover whose papers are not complete, and taking a test booklet may be grounds for disqualification.

VIII. EXAMINATION TECHNIQUES

1) Read the general instructions carefully. These are usually printed on the first page of the exam booklet. As a rule, these instructions refer to the timing of the examination; the fact that you should not start work until the signal and must stop work at a signal, etc. If there are any *special* instructions, such as a choice of questions to be answered, make sure that you note this instruction carefully.

2) When you are ready to start work on the examination, that is as soon as the signal has been given, read the instructions to each question booklet, underline any key words or phrases, such as *least, best, outline, describe* and the like. In this way you will tend to answer as requested rather than discover on reviewing your paper that you *listed without describing*, that you selected the *worst* choice rather than the *best* choice, etc.

3) If the examination is of the objective or multiple-choice type – that is, each question will also give a series of possible answers: A, B, C or D, and you are called upon to select the best answer and write the letter next to that answer on your answer paper – it is advisable to start answering each question in turn. There may be anywhere from 50 to 100 such questions in the three or four hours allotted and you can see how much time would be taken if you read through all the questions before beginning to answer any. Furthermore, if you come across a question or group of questions which you know would be difficult to answer, it would undoubtedly affect your handling of all the other questions.

4) If the examination is of the essay type and contains but a few questions, it is a moot point as to whether you should read all the questions before starting to answer any one. Of course, if you are given a choice – say five out of seven and the like – then it is essential to read all the questions so you can eliminate the two that are most difficult. If, however, you are asked to answer all the questions, there may be danger in trying to answer the easiest one first because you may find that you will spend too much time on it. The best technique is to answer the first question, then proceed to the second, etc.

5) Time your answers. Before the exam begins, write down the time it started, then add the time allowed for the examination and write down the time it must be completed, then divide the time available somewhat as follows:
   - If 3-1/2 hours are allowed, that would be 210 minutes. If you have 80 objective-type questions, that would be an average of 2-1/2 minutes per question. Allow yourself no more than 2 minutes per question, or a total of 160 minutes, which will permit about 50 minutes to review.
   - If for the time allotment of 210 minutes there are 7 essay questions to answer, that would average about 30 minutes a question. Give yourself only 25 minutes per question so that you have about 35 minutes to review.

6) The most important instruction is to *read each question* and make sure you know what is wanted. The second most important instruction is to *time yourself properly* so that you answer every question. The third most important instruction is to *answer every question.* Guess if you have to but include something for each question. Remember that you will receive no credit for a blank and will probably receive some credit if you write something in answer to an essay question. If you guess a letter – say "B" for a multiple-choice question – you may have guessed right. If you leave a blank as an answer to a multiple-choice question, the examiners may respect your feelings but it will not add a point to your score. Some exams may penalize you for wrong answers, so in such cases *only*, you may not want to guess unless you have some basis for your answer.

7) Suggestions
   a. Objective-type questions
      1. Examine the question booklet for proper sequence of pages and questions
      2. Read all instructions carefully
      3. Skip any question which seems too difficult; return to it after all other questions have been answered
      4. Apportion your time properly; do not spend too much time on any single question or group of questions

5. Note and underline key words – *all, most, fewest, least, best, worst, same, opposite,* etc.
6. Pay particular attention to negatives
7. Note unusual option, e.g., unduly long, short, complex, different or similar in content to the body of the question
8. Observe the use of "hedging" words – *probably, may, most likely,* etc.
9. Make sure that your answer is put next to the same number as the question
10. Do not second-guess unless you have good reason to believe the second answer is definitely more correct
11. Cross out original answer if you decide another answer is more accurate; do not erase until you are ready to hand your paper in
12. Answer all questions; guess unless instructed otherwise
13. Leave time for review

b. Essay questions

1. Read each question carefully
2. Determine exactly what is wanted. Underline key words or phrases.
3. Decide on outline or paragraph answer
4. Include many different points and elements unless asked to develop any one or two points or elements
5. Show impartiality by giving pros and cons unless directed to select one side only
6. Make and write down any assumptions you find necessary to answer the questions
7. Watch your English, grammar, punctuation and choice of words
8. Time your answers; don't crowd material

8) Answering the essay question

Most essay questions can be answered by framing the specific response around several key words or ideas. Here are a few such key words or ideas:

M's: manpower, materials, methods, money, management
P's: purpose, program, policy, plan, procedure, practice, problems, pitfalls, personnel, public relations

a. Six basic steps in handling problems:

1. Preliminary plan and background development
2. Collect information, data and facts
3. Analyze and interpret information, data and facts
4. Analyze and develop solutions as well as make recommendations
5. Prepare report and sell recommendations
6. Install recommendations and follow up effectiveness

b. Pitfalls to avoid

1. *Taking things for granted* – A statement of the situation does not necessarily imply that each of the elements is necessarily true; for example, a complaint may be invalid and biased so that all that can be taken for granted is that a complaint has been registered

2. *Considering only one side of a situation* – Wherever possible, indicate several alternatives and then point out the reasons you selected the best one
3. *Failing to indicate follow up* – Whenever your answer indicates action on your part, make certain that you will take proper follow-up action to see how successful your recommendations, procedures or actions turn out to be
4. *Taking too long in answering any single question* – Remember to time your answers properly

IX. AFTER THE TEST

Scoring procedures differ in detail among civil service jurisdictions although the general principles are the same. Whether the papers are hand-scored or graded by machine we have described, they are nearly always graded by number. That is, the person who marks the paper knows only the number – never the name – of the applicant. Not until all the papers have been graded will they be matched with names. If other tests, such as training and experience or oral interview ratings have been given, scores will be combined. Different parts of the examination usually have different weights. For example, the written test might count 60 percent of the final grade, and a rating of training and experience 40 percent. In many jurisdictions, veterans will have a certain number of points added to their grades.

After the final grade has been determined, the names are placed in grade order and an eligible list is established. There are various methods for resolving ties between those who get the same final grade – probably the most common is to place first the name of the person whose application was received first. Job offers are made from the eligible list in the order the names appear on it. You will be notified of your grade and your rank as soon as all these computations have been made. This will be done as rapidly as possible.

People who are found to meet the requirements in the announcement are called "eligibles." Their names are put on a list of eligible candidates. An eligible's chances of getting a job depend on how high he stands on this list and how fast agencies are filling jobs from the list.

When a job is to be filled from a list of eligibles, the agency asks for the names of people on the list of eligibles for that job. When the civil service commission receives this request, it sends to the agency the names of the three people highest on this list. Or, if the job to be filled has specialized requirements, the office sends the agency the names of the top three persons who meet these requirements from the general list.

The appointing officer makes a choice from among the three people whose names were sent to him. If the selected person accepts the appointment, the names of the others are put back on the list to be considered for future openings.

That is the rule in hiring from all kinds of eligible lists, whether they are for typist, carpenter, chemist, or something else. For every vacancy, the appointing officer has his choice of any one of the top three eligibles on the list. This explains why the person whose name is on top of the list sometimes does not get an appointment when some of the persons lower on the list do. If the appointing officer chooses the second or third eligible, the No. 1 eligible does not get a job at once, but stays on the list until he is appointed or the list is terminated.

X. HOW TO PASS THE INTERVIEW TEST

The examination for which you applied requires an oral interview test. You have already taken the written test and you are now being called for the interview test – the final part of the formal examination.

You may think that it is not possible to prepare for an interview test and that there are no procedures to follow during an interview. Our purpose is to point out some things you can do in advance that will help you and some good rules to follow and pitfalls to avoid while you are being interviewed.

What is an interview supposed to test?

The written examination is designed to test the technical knowledge and competence of the candidate; the oral is designed to evaluate intangible qualities, not readily measured otherwise, and to establish a list showing the relative fitness of each candidate – as measured against his competitors – for the position sought. Scoring is not on the basis of "right" and "wrong," but on a sliding scale of values ranging from "not passable" to "outstanding." As a matter of fact, it is possible to achieve a relatively low score without a single "incorrect" answer because of evident weakness in the qualities being measured.

Occasionally, an examination may consist entirely of an oral test – either an individual or a group oral. In such cases, information is sought concerning the technical knowledges and abilities of the candidate, since there has been no written examination for this purpose. More commonly, however, an oral test is used to supplement a written examination.

Who conducts interviews?

The composition of oral boards varies among different jurisdictions. In nearly all, a representative of the personnel department serves as chairman. One of the members of the board may be a representative of the department in which the candidate would work. In some cases, "outside experts" are used, and, frequently, a businessman or some other representative of the general public is asked to serve. Labor and management or other special groups may be represented. The aim is to secure the services of experts in the appropriate field.

However the board is composed, it is a good idea (and not at all improper or unethical) to ascertain in advance of the interview who the members are and what groups they represent. When you are introduced to them, you will have some idea of their backgrounds and interests, and at least you will not stutter and stammer over their names.

What should be done before the interview?

While knowledge about the board members is useful and takes some of the surprise element out of the interview, there is other preparation which is more substantive. It *is* possible to prepare for an oral interview – in several ways:

1) Keep a copy of your application and review it carefully before the interview

This may be the only document before the oral board, and the starting point of the interview. Know what education and experience you have listed there, and the sequence and dates of all of it. Sometimes the board will ask you to review the highlights of your experience for them; you should not have to hem and haw doing it.

2) Study the class specification and the examination announcement

Usually, the oral board has one or both of these to guide them. The qualities, characteristics or knowledges required by the position sought are stated in these documents. They offer valuable clues as to the nature of the oral interview. For example, if the job involves supervisory responsibilities, the announcement will usually indicate that knowledge of modern supervisory methods and the qualifications of the candidate as a supervisor will be tested. If so, you can expect such questions, frequently in the form of a hypothetical situation which you are expected to solve. NEVER go into an oral without knowledge of the duties and responsibilities of the job you seek.

3) Think through each qualification required

Try to visualize the kind of questions you would ask if you were a board member. How well could you answer them? Try especially to appraise your own knowledge and background in each area, *measured against the job sought*, and identify any areas in which you are weak. Be critical and realistic – do not flatter yourself.

4) Do some general reading in areas in which you feel you may be weak

For example, if the job involves supervision and your past experience has NOT, some general reading in supervisory methods and practices, particularly in the field of human relations, might be useful. Do NOT study agency procedures or detailed manuals. The oral board will be testing your understanding and capacity, not your memory.

5) Get a good night's sleep and watch your general health and mental attitude

You will want a clear head at the interview. Take care of a cold or any other minor ailment, and of course, no hangovers.

What should be done on the day of the interview?

Now comes the day of the interview itself. Give yourself plenty of time to get there. Plan to arrive somewhat ahead of the scheduled time, particularly if your appointment is in the fore part of the day. If a previous candidate fails to appear, the board might be ready for you a bit early. By early afternoon an oral board is almost invariably behind schedule if there are many candidates, and you may have to wait. Take along a book or magazine to read, or your application to review, but leave any extraneous material in the waiting room when you go in for your interview. In any event, relax and compose yourself.

The matter of dress is important. The board is forming impressions about you – from your experience, your manners, your attitude, and your appearance. Give your personal appearance careful attention. Dress your best, but not your flashiest. Choose conservative, appropriate clothing, and be sure it is immaculate. This is a business interview, and your appearance should indicate that you regard it as such. Besides, being well groomed and properly dressed will help boost your confidence.

Sooner or later, someone will call your name and escort you into the interview room. *This is it.* From here on you are on your own. It is too late for any more preparation. But remember, you asked for this opportunity to prove your fitness, and you are here because your request was granted.

What happens when you go in?

The usual sequence of events will be as follows: The clerk (who is often the board stenographer) will introduce you to the chairman of the oral board, who will introduce you to the other members of the board. Acknowledge the introductions before you sit down. Do not be surprised if you find a microphone facing you or a stenotypist sitting by. Oral interviews are usually recorded in the event of an appeal or other review.

Usually the chairman of the board will open the interview by reviewing the highlights of your education and work experience from your application – primarily for the benefit of the other members of the board, as well as to get the material into the record. Do not interrupt or comment unless there is an error or significant misinterpretation; if that is the case, do not hesitate. But do not quibble about insignificant matters. Also, he will usually ask you some question about your education, experience or your present job – partly to get you to start talking and to establish the interviewing "rapport." He may start the actual questioning, or turn it over to one of the other members. Frequently, each member undertakes the questioning on a particular area, one in which he is perhaps most competent, so you can expect each member to participate in the examination. Because time is limited, you may also expect some rather abrupt switches in the direction the questioning takes, so do not be upset by it. Normally, a board member will not pursue a single line of questioning unless he discovers a particular strength or weakness.

After each member has participated, the chairman will usually ask whether any member has any further questions, then will ask you if you have anything you wish to add. Unless you are expecting this question, it may floor you. Worse, it may start you off on an extended, extemporaneous speech. The board is not usually seeking more information. The question is principally to offer you a last opportunity to present further qualifications or to indicate that you have nothing to add. So, if you feel that a significant qualification or characteristic has been overlooked, it is proper to point it out in a sentence or so. Do not compliment the board on the thoroughness of their examination – they have been sketchy, and you know it. If you wish, merely say, "No thank you, I have nothing further to add." This is a point where you can "talk yourself out" of a good impression or fail to present an important bit of information. Remember, *you close the interview yourself.*

The chairman will then say, "That is all, Mr. ______, thank you." Do not be startled; the interview is over, and quicker than you think. Thank him, gather your belongings and take your leave. Save your sigh of relief for the other side of the door.

How to put your best foot forward

Throughout this entire process, you may feel that the board individually and collectively is trying to pierce your defenses, seek out your hidden weaknesses and embarrass and confuse you. Actually, this is not true. They are obliged to make an appraisal of your qualifications for the job you are seeking, and they want to see you in your best light. Remember, they must interview all candidates and a non-cooperative candidate may become a failure in spite of their best efforts to bring out his qualifications. Here are 15 suggestions that will help you:

1) Be natural – Keep your attitude confident, not cocky

If you are not confident that you can do the job, do not expect the board to be. Do not apologize for your weaknesses, try to bring out your strong points. The board is interested in a positive, not negative, presentation. Cockiness will antagonize any board member and make him wonder if you are covering up a weakness by a false show of strength.

2) Get comfortable, but don't lounge or sprawl

Sit erectly but not stiffly. A careless posture may lead the board to conclude that you are careless in other things, or at least that you are not impressed by the importance of the occasion. Either conclusion is natural, even if incorrect. Do not fuss with your clothing, a pencil or an ashtray. Your hands may occasionally be useful to emphasize a point; do not let them become a point of distraction.

3) Do not wisecrack or make small talk

This is a serious situation, and your attitude should show that you consider it as such. Further, the time of the board is limited – they do not want to waste it, and neither should you.

4) Do not exaggerate your experience or abilities

In the first place, from information in the application or other interviews and sources, the board may know more about you than you think. Secondly, you probably will not get away with it. An experienced board is rather adept at spotting such a situation, so do not take the chance.

5) If you know a board member, do not make a point of it, yet do not hide it

Certainly you are not fooling him, and probably not the other members of the board. Do not try to take advantage of your acquaintanceship – it will probably do you little good.

6) Do not dominate the interview

Let the board do that. They will give you the clues – do not assume that you have to do all the talking. Realize that the board has a number of questions to ask you, and do not try to take up all the interview time by showing off your extensive knowledge of the answer to the first one.

7) Be attentive

You only have 20 minutes or so, and you should keep your attention at its sharpest throughout. When a member is addressing a problem or question to you, give him your undivided attention. Address your reply principally to him, but do not exclude the other board members.

8) Do not interrupt

A board member may be stating a problem for you to analyze. He will ask you a question when the time comes. Let him state the problem, and wait for the question.

9) Make sure you understand the question

Do not try to answer until you are sure what the question is. If it is not clear, restate it in your own words or ask the board member to clarify it for you. However, do not haggle about minor elements.

10) Reply promptly but not hastily

A common entry on oral board rating sheets is "candidate responded readily," or "candidate hesitated in replies." Respond as promptly and quickly as you can, but do not jump to a hasty, ill-considered answer.

11) Do not be peremptory in your answers

A brief answer is proper – but do not fire your answer back. That is a losing game from your point of view. The board member can probably ask questions much faster than you can answer them.

12) Do not try to create the answer you think the board member wants

He is interested in what kind of mind you have and how it works – not in playing games. Furthermore, he can usually spot this practice and will actually grade you down on it.

13) Do not switch sides in your reply merely to agree with a board member

Frequently, a member will take a contrary position merely to draw you out and to see if you are willing and able to defend your point of view. Do not start a debate, yet do not surrender a good position. If a position is worth taking, it is worth defending.

14) Do not be afraid to admit an error in judgment if you are shown to be wrong

The board knows that you are forced to reply without any opportunity for careful consideration. Your answer may be demonstrably wrong. If so, admit it and get on with the interview.

15) Do not dwell at length on your present job

The opening question may relate to your present assignment. Answer the question but do not go into an extended discussion. You are being examined for a *new* job, not your present one. As a matter of fact, try to phrase ALL your answers in terms of the job for which you are being examined.

Basis of Rating

Probably you will forget most of these "do's" and "don'ts" when you walk into the oral interview room. Even remembering them all will not ensure you a passing grade. Perhaps you did not have the qualifications in the first place. But remembering them will help you to put your best foot forward, without treading on the toes of the board members.

Rumor and popular opinion to the contrary notwithstanding, an oral board wants you to make the best appearance possible. They know you are under pressure – but they also want to see how you respond to it as a guide to what your reaction would be under the pressures of the job you seek. They will be influenced by the degree of poise you display, the personal traits you show and the manner in which you respond.

ABOUT THIS BOOK

This book contains tests divided into Examination Sections. Go through each test, answering every question in the margin. We have also attached a sample answer sheet at the back of the book that can be removed and used. At the end of each test look at the answer key and check your answers. On the ones you got wrong, look at the right answer choice and learn. Do not fill in the answers first. Do not memorize the questions and answers, but understand the answer and principles involved. On your test, the questions will likely be different from the samples. Questions are changed and new ones added. If you understand these past questions you should have success with any changes that arise. Tests may consist of several types of questions. We have additional books on each subject should more study be advisable or necessary for you. Finally, the more you study, the better prepared you will be. This book is intended to be the last thing you study before you walk into the examination room. Prior study of relevant texts is also recommended. NLC publishes some of these in our Fundamental Series. Knowledge and good sense are important factors in passing your exam. Good luck also helps. So now study this Passbook, absorb the material contained within and take that knowledge into the examination. Then do your best to pass that exam.

———

EXAMINATION SECTION

EXAMINATION SECTION
TEST 1

DIRECTIONS: Each question or incomplete statement is followed by several suggested answers or completions. Select the one that BEST answers the question or completes the statement. *PRINT THE LETTER OF THE CORRECT ANSWER IN THE SPACE AT THE RIGHT.*

1. The shift from an individual to a formal response of crime resulted in which one of the following: 1.____

   A. Elimination of revenge
   B. Made punishment more humane
   C. Lessened the chances of longstanding family feuds
   D. Promoted citizen disinterest in crime and the punishment of criminals
   E. Contributed to the development of a more just method of determining guilt

2. The MOST important trend in corrections today: 2.____

   A. Attempt to reinforce any ties between the offender and the community
   B. Long sentences
   C. Less use of confinement if possible
   D. Developing programs for prisoners in prisons
   E. None of the above

3. People commit crimes because 3.____

   A. they are mentally ill
   B. they come from poor families
   C. it is their way of trying to solve their problems
   D. they want to
   E. they are born criminals

4. The jail officer's role in the jail is to 4.____

   I. represent the sheriff
   II. represent the criminal justice system
   III. assume responsibility for the welfare of prisoners
   IV. punish prisoners for their crimes
   V. appease social pressure

   The CORRECT answer is:

   A. I, II B. II, III C. I, II, III
   D. II, III, IV E. II, V

5. Which one of the following is a *genuine* characteristic of a professional jail officer? He 5.____

   A. becomes easily upset by prisoners
   B. wants to punish prisoners for their crimes
   C. tries to treat all prisoners alike without favoritism or emotion
   D. refuses to discuss the prisoners' guilt or innocence
   E. is critical of the courts and the law and says so to prisoners

KEY (CORRECT ANSWERS)

1. E
2. A
3. C
4. B
5. C

TEST 2

DIRECTIONS: Each question or incomplete statement is followed by several suggested answers or completions. Select the one that BEST answers the question or completes the statement. *PRINT THE LETTER OF THE CORRECT ANSWER IN THE SPACE AT THE RIGHT.*

1. From the list below, select the one that is legally proper on which the jail officer can book a prisoner: 1.____

   A. Larceny
   B. Hold for Dr. Jones
   C. False identification
   D. Suspicion
   E. Hold for investigation

2. The purpose of a strip search is: 2.____
   I. To discover contraband
   II. To let the prisoner know that he is now in jail
   III. To discover if he has lice
   IV. To appraise physical condition
   V. All of the above

   The CORRECT answer is:

   A. I, II
   B. II, III
   C. I, IV
   D. I, III
   E. V

3. Select those statements that are TRUE about strip and frisk searches: 3.____
   I. If you are not certain that you examined an area, return to it
   II. All searches should be systematic
   III. An incomplete search is as bad as no search at all
   IV. Your attitude when conducting the search is as important as the way the search is done
   V. All of the above

   The CORRECT answer is:

   A. I, III
   B. II, III
   C. II, III, IV
   D. I, III, IV
   E. V

4. Identification procedures are important because: 4.____
   I. The FBI requires them
   II. It is a method of identifying those persons who are wanted by other jurisdictions
   III. It is a method of identifying prisoners when they are released
   IV. It is necessary for statistical purposes
   V. All of the above

   The CORRECT answer is:

   A. II, III
   B. I, IV
   C. II, IV
   D. I, II
   E. V

5. Physical examinations for all prisoners at the time of admission are 5.____

   A. a waste of time since most of them are drunks anyway
   B. necessary to discover the sick and injured
   C. necessary only if a prisoner seems to be obviously sick
   D. duplicatory of previous physicals

6. Which of the following are NOT accurate descriptions of personal property and should not be used? 6.____

   I. Gold watch
   II. Plaid sport coat, size 40
   III. Yellow metal ring with diamond
   IV. Brown suit, Bonds label, hole in left elbow, trousers soiled at right knee, size 40
   V. Timex watch

   The CORRECT answer is:

   A. I, II, V
   B. II, III, V
   C. I, IV, V
   D. I, II, III
   E. I, III, V

7. Bathing of all prisoners when they are admitted to the jail is necessary for the following reasons: 7.____

   I. It is good for staff morale to see clean prisoners
   II. Prevent vermin from entering the jail
   III. No one likes dirty people
   IV. It contributes to the health and well-being of prisoners
   V. All of the above

   The CORRECT answer is:

   A. I, II
   B. II, III
   C. III, IV
   D. II, IV
   E. V

8. Prisoners should not be permitted to wear long hair because 8.____

   A. it is unsightly
   B. it is unsanitary
   C. the jail staff do not like it
   D. all of the above
   E. none of the above

9. All prisoners should wear jail clothing because 9.____

   A. they look neater when they all are dressed alike
   B. it is a good security procedure since it makes escape difficult
   C. it is simpler for them to do their laundry
   D. it is cheaper

10. Match the following descriptions of prisoners with the appropriate housing assignment: 10.

A.	Juvenile prisoner	1.	dormitory, near infirmary	A.____
B.	Elderly or infirm prisoner	2.	in single cell away from all adults	B.____
C.	Mentally ill prisoner	3.	in a single cell	C.____
D.	Hostile aggressive prisoner	4.	in a single cell under close supervision	D.____
		5.	in a padded cell	

11. The PROPER definition of contraband is: 11.____

A. Any item that can be used as a weapon, and all drugs
B. All items listed as contraband and posted in the jail
C. All items not issued by the jail and not specifically authorized
D. Illicit guns.

12. Cell searches are necessary for the following reason: 12.____

A. To discover contraband
B. To keep prisoners off balance
C. To reduce clutter
D. All of the above

13. Identify the two MOST important principles of a cell search: 13.____

I. Examine everything in the cell
II. Be systematic
III. Leave the cell in the same condition in which it was found
IV. Ignore the prisoner when searching his cell
V. Remain aloof

The CORRECT answer is:

A. I, II
B. II, III
C. III, IV
D. IV, V
E. I, III

14. Indicate whether the following statements are TRUE or FALSE: 14.

A. Counts are unnecessary if prisoners are locked up at all times. A.____
B. A jail officer should know how many prisoners he has at all times. B.____
C. One officer can make an accurate count in a dormitory. C.____
D. Roll call counts are easy to take and make good sense. D.____
E. When counting prisoners, the officer must always see flesh. E.____
F. It is not good practice to permit prisoners to conduct a count F.____

15. Select the statements that are examples of good key control: 15.____

I. Since minimum security prisoners can be trusted, it is proper to permit them to use keys to unlock and lock all doors
II. A jail officer should never carry both inside and outside keys
III. Jail officers should be permitted to exchange keys during shift change
IV. All security keys should be concealed when carried
V. None of the above

The CORRECT answer is:

A. I, III
B. II, III
C. II, IV
D. I, IV
E. V

16. The single MOST effective security measure in the jail is 16.____

A. remote TV camera
B. tool-hardened steel
C. metal detectors
D. the alertness of the jail officer
E. stoolies

17. Indicate whether the following statements are TRUE or FALSE: 17.

A. Weapons are needed in the jail in order to protect personnel A.____
B. Gas in aerosol cans and clubs are not weapons B.____
C. The weapon carried in the jail by the officer can be taken away and used against him C.____
D. Although all jail personnel should be required to check their weapons before entering the jail, FBI agents and visiting sheriffs are exempt D.____
E. The armory should be inside the jail so that weapons will be available to jail officers when they need them E.____

KEY (CORRECT ANSWERS)

1. A
2. D
3. C
4. A
5. B

6. E
7. D
8. E
9. B
10. A. 2
    B. 1
    C. 4
    D. 3

11. C
12. A
13. B
14. A. F
    B. T
    C. F
    D. F
    E. T
    F. T
15. C

16. D
17. A. F
    B. F
    C. T
    D. F
    E. F

TEST 3

DIRECTIONS: Each question or incomplete statement is followed by several suggested answers or completions. Select the one that BEST answers the question or completes the statement. *PRINT THE LETTER OF THE CORRECT ANSWER IN THE SPACE AT THE RIGHT.*

1. What are the two MOST important changes that occur when a prisoner is admitted to the jail? He 1.____

   A. becomes a prisoner
   B. changes status from citizen to prisoner
   C. has to wear jail clothing
   D. begins to lose his identity

2. List the *tangible* items that contribute to a prisoner's identity and that are taken from him when he enters the jail. (List six.) 2.____

   1. ____________ 2. ____________
   3. ____________ 4. ____________
   5. ____________ 6. ____________

3. List the *intangibles* that contribute to a prisoner's identity that he loses when he enters the jail. (List three.) 3.____

   1. ____________ 2. ____________ 3. ____________

4. Indicate whether the following statements are TRUE or FALSE: 4.

   A. Prisoners are generally not frustrated by their inability to do things for themselves because they have few things bothering them. A.____
   B. Giving a prisoner good conduct time is equal to rewards he would receive in the community such as pay, approval, and responsibility. B.____
   C. Cutting a prisoner's hair at admission does not alter his identity. C.____
   D. A prisoner's sudden dependence on his wife and friends does not change his relationship with them. D.____
   E. There is no similarity between the feelings a prisoner has when confined and the person who is entering military service. E.____

5. The newly admitted prisoner can be assisted in adjusting to the jail by one of the following methods: 5.____

   A. Orientation by other prisoners
   B. Written rules and regulations that are given to him
   C. Trial and error and by watching others
   D. Kept in a cell until he learns jail routine

6. Although any period in confinement can be considered a critical time, the following times are especially sensitive: (Select two.) 6.____

   A. During discharge of the prisoner from the jail
   B. During searches of cells
   C. During strip or frisk searches
   D. Immediately before or after court appearances
   E. During mealtimes
   F. All of the above

7. What should be done about a prisoner who appears hostile during admission? 7.____

A. Lock him up in a cell immediately
B. Insist on carrying out the admission procedure and ask the arresting officer to assist you
C. Be certain to get all the details of the arrest and the prisoner's behavior from the arresting officer. This should be done in the presence of the prisoner so that he knows he can't fool you.
D. Get rid of the arresting officer as soon as possible. Carry out the admission procedure calmly and quietly.

8. The BEST procedure to follow when a prisoner is upset from a visit from his wife or girlfriend is to do the following: 8.____

A. Lock him in a cell by himself so that he will not try to escape and where he will not disturb others
B. Permit him to call his wife or girlfriend and correct the misunderstanding
C. Talk to the prisoner or at least be a sympathetic and understanding listener
D. If he is continuously having problems because of argument with visitors, refuse to let further visits to take place

9. Although many factors are involved in setting and controlling the jail climate, the MOST important is: 9.____

A. The behavior of the prisoners since they can be hostile and manipulative
B. The attitude and behavior of the staff
C. The quality of the food
D. Relaxed security procedures
E. All of the above

10. The following technique is useful in avoiding prisoner manipulation: 10.____

A. Refuse to discuss any prisoner's problems with him
B. Establish good communications with other staff members
C. Keep good records
D. Ignore prisoner complaints and refuse to permit any exceptions to jail rules

11. Indicate whether the following statements are TRUE or FALSE: 11.

A. A suicide attempt is usually an attempt to manipulate jail staff A.____
B. Overreacting to prisoners is an indication that the jail officer is conscientious and concerned B.____
C. A jail officer should always act knowledgeable about jail procedures even when he is not C.____
D. Jail rules seldom need to be changed; they do need to be updated by adding new rules from time to time D.____
E. There is nothing wrong with rules made up by prisoners because usually they are tougher than rules developed by the administrator E.____

12. A jail officer who overreacts to prisoners is 12.____

A. alert to prisoner manipulation
B. demonstrating an interest in his work
C. lacks confidence and is insecure
D. all of the above

13. List characteristics of the trained, professional jailer: (List seven.) 13.____

1. ____________ 2. ____________
3. ____________ 4. ____________
5. ____________ 6. ____________
7. ____________

14. Indicate whether the following statements are TRUE or FALSE: 14.

A. A jail officer who disagrees with a jail rule and lets prisoners know it will be considered an honest officer and will be contributing to a positive jail climate A.____
B. The jail officer who gossips with prisoners gets their respect because he is demonstrating that he is just like they are B.____
C. Discussing dissatisfactions about the jail with prisoners is a good way to get good suggestions for changes in jail policy C.____
D. Prisoners are quick to interpret differences of opinion between staff members as signs of disunity D.____
E. Regulations assist prisoners in adjusting to the jail by eliminating confusion E.____
F. Rigid rules are the most effective way of keeping order and contribute to a well-run jail and few disciplinary reports F.____
G. Vague regulations are an indication to prisoners that personnel do not have clear understanding or control of the jail G.____
H. Reasonable rules reduce staff-prisoner conflict H.____

KEY (CORRECT ANSWERS)

1. B, D
2. Street clothing, haircut, jewelry, belt, tie clip, cigarette lighter
3. Work, relations with his family, daily habits
4. A. F
   B. F
   C. F
   D. F
   E. F
5. B
6. C, D
7. D
8. C
9. B
10. B
11. A. F
    B. F
    C. F
    D. F
    E. F
12. C
13. Flexibility, self-confidence, willingness to make decisions, impartiality, refusal to respond in a hostile manner to prisoner hostility, respect for himself and his work, willingness to perform all necessary tasks
14. A. F
    B. F
    C. F
    D. T
    E. T
    F. F
    G. T
    H. T

TEST 4

DIRECTIONS: Each question or incomplete statement is followed by several suggested answers or completions. Select the one that BEST answers the question or completes the statement. *PRINT THE LETTER OF THE CORRECT ANSWER IN THE SPACE AT THE RIGHT.*

1. Select the one statement that completes the following sentence. 1.____
The overall objective of supervision is

   A. achievement of security
   B. protection of prisoners
   C. teaching prisoners how to work
   D. the development of an orderly environment

2. Another important goal of supervision is control. This means: 2.____

   A. Making certain that each prisoner is either locked in his cell or under the direct physical control of the jail officer
   B. That jail officers closely supervise prisoner activities, especially where trusties are in charge of other prisoners
   C. That jail personnel supervise all prisoners, develop procedures, set standards, and evaluate results
   D. All of the above

3. An officer is placed on a new assignment where he will be supervising prisoners. 3.____
Which of the following is the proper FIRST step he should take in assuming this assignment?

   A. Call the prisoners together and tell them what kind of work he expects from them.
   B. Ask the prisoners for suggestions on how this particular operation can be improved.
   C. Ask each prisoner for a description of his work so that he can seek ways to revise procedures and make them more effective.
   D. Read post orders, familiarize himself with policies and procedures, and learn all he can about the assignment.

4. Officer P assigned four prisoners to a small empty cell block and gave them the following instructions. *I want this place cleaned up. I'll be back before the end of the day to check on your work.* 4.____
List the errors made by Officer P. (List three.)

   1. ______________________________
   2. ______________________________
   3. ______________________________

5. A supervisor is responsible for making an accurate and honest evaluation of a prisoner's performance. 5.____
In order to do this, he must

   A. know a great deal about the prisoner, including his offense, his family life, and his education
   B. have supervised him long enough to know him well

C. recognize and account for individual differences
D. evaluate all prisoners as working equally hard or satisfactorily
E. recognize either improvement or a change for the worse and, if possible, explain it

6. Select the two statements that demonstrate a supervisor's objectivity in evaluating a prisoner: 6._____

A. This man is lazy
B. This man is always at the end of the line when picking up tools and first in line when turning them in
C. Prisoner J is one of the slowest moving men in the crew
D. Prisoner A is hard working, energetic, and always on the go
E. Prisoner S listens carefully, asks questions when he does not understand, and makes few mistakes

7. Officer R is trying hard to do a good job. He feels that it is important for jail officers to communicate with prisoners. In this way, he can keep in touch with them and their problems and, as a result, will be a more effective supervisor. This morning he came in and in talking to some of the prisoners commented that he certainly was tired; he should not have stayed out so late. Not only was he tired, but his wife was angry with him because of the late hours he keeps when bowling. 7._____
One of the prisoners asked him about his score. He replied that he averaged 105. One of the prisoners commented that this was a lady's score, and the other prisoners laughed.
What errors did Officer R make? (List three.)

1. ______________________________
2. ______________________________
3. ______________________________

8. Officer S has been talking to Prisoner O. During the conversation, O says, *"Don't you think that Idiot T would know better than to loan I cigarettes when he knows I is leaving before commissary day?"* Officer S replied, *"I never did think T had too many brains and now I'm certain of it. But then, I doesn't have too many smarts either."* What do you think Prisoner O is thinking of Officer S's remarks? (Select one.) 8._____

A. Well, we seem to agree about some things.
B. Gee, Officer S is pretty sharp about who is smart or dumb.
C. I wonder what he says about me to other prisoners.
D. He is right about T but I think I is a smart old bird. But I'm not going to argue with him.

9. Prisoner B is having problems with his wife. She wants to have their eight-year-old boy's tonsils removed, and B wants her to wait until he is released. He is discussing the problem with Officer R who tells him, *"Listen, "let her have them removed. The sooner the better; it's like pulling a tooth, fast and simple."* 9._____
Do you think this advice was good or bad? (Select one.)

A. *Good;* it will keep the wife occupied while Prisoner B is in jail.
B. *Good;* the boy should have his tonsils removed.
C. *Bad;* Officer R knows nothing about the family situation or the boy's medical condition.

D. *Bad;* he is taking the wife's side in the argument.
E. *Good;* he is giving the prisoner advice, and the prisoner needs it if he is to resolve his problem.

10. The Lockmeup County Jail is run simply and with little fuss or bother. The sheriff has found that the prisoners can pretty well take care of themselves. The jail is fairly clean and seems to be quite orderly. It seems, however, that some prisoners never do any work and always have money, cigarettes, and commissary. 10.____
What is going on here?

A. The prisoners are probably a well-behaved, cooperative group who are interested in getting along with the sheriff.
B. It is highly probable that prisoners are running the jail and have established a sanitary court.
C. Both of the above
D. None of the above

11. Officer J has assigned three prisoners to the kitchen detail to wash pots, mop the floor, and wipe tables. He will not be available to supervise them at all times. He has, therefore, given one of the prisoners responsibility for organizing the work and giving out assignments. 11.____
Is Officer J making any supervisory errors?

A. *No;* a good supervisor learns to delegate responsibility.
B. *Yes;* prisoners should never have any supervisory responsibility over other prisoners.
C. *No;* he will be checking them from time to time so there is little chance that anything will go wrong.
D. *Yes;* he has not been clear in his assignment of work.

12. Officer P is responsible for the supervision of a cell block during the evening hours when there is little activity in the jail. His post is at the door to the cell block, but he makes it a habit to make rounds of the cell block once every hour. His tour always takes place during the last 15 minutes of the hour. Officer P believes in being systematic and organized. This evening Prisoner S asked him for a light and engaged him in conversation. S is usually not talkative. The other prisoners lounging in the bullpen area between cells seemed somewhat noisier than usual, but not to the point where it would be disturbing. 12.____
What do you think could be happening in the cell block?

A. Nothing; it is not unusual for prisoners to change and become friendly. In fact, S's desire to talk should be encouraged; perhaps in time he may want to discuss his problems with Officer P.
B. An escape is in progress, and the prisoners are trying to provide a distraction.
C. These distractions could cover an escape attempt or sexual assaults in another part of the jail.
D. Nothing; the prisoner usually becomes a little noisy as the evening progresses.

13. Referring to Question 12 above, do you think Officer P is making any errors? 13.____

A. *No;* he is responding to a prisoner's need to talk to someone.
B. *Yes;* he should not make his tours through the cell block according to such a rigid schedule.

C. *No*; he seems to be alert and is actively supervising the cell block.
D. *Yes;* he should not be giving S a light.

14. The television set for prisoners is located in the day-room. Although it had been possible to buy the set with remote controls, this was not done. 14.____
How do you think the jail staff can ensure that they will exercise control over the set?
I. The threat of losing the television will be enough to keep the prisoners in line.
II. The on-off switch should be controlled by the jail staff.
III. The prisoners should be permitted to set up a committee to develop rules for television use.
IV. Jail staff should set viewing hours and have the final approval over programs.
The CORRECT answer is:

A. I, II B. II, III C. I, IV
D. III, IV E. II, IV

15. The jail is switching over to dining room feeding. This has been made possible by the addition of eight jail officers. 15.____
Where should the posts be located to cover the trouble spots?
A. Along the walls of the dining room
B. Circulating in the dining room
C. One watching the line entering the dining room, one in the kitchen, and the other circulating
D. One at the line entering the dining room, one at the serving line, one at the silverware collection and tray scraping can, and three either along the wall or circulating

16. List the important points in supervising the feeding of prisoners in their cells. (List four.) 16.____
1. ____________________
2. ____________________
3. ____________________
4. ____________________

17. Although the jail has a routine procedure for handling sick call, Officer P has worked out a much simpler system. Whenever a prisoner requests to see the doctor, Officer P questions him; and if the prisoner complains of a headache or cold, he is given two aspirin. This has reduced the sick call line substantially. Officer P prides himself in his ability to handle sick call requests and to spot the chronic complainers. 17.____
Do you feel that Officer P's behavior is proper?
I. No; jail officers should not give out medication.
II. Yes; doctors are busy and reducing the number of sick call requests will help them give more time to those who are really sick.
III. No; Officer P is diagnosing prisoner medical complaints, and he is not qualified to do this.
IV. Yes, as long as he limits his medical activity to those who have colds and headaches.
V. Yes; after all, the prisoners are diagnosing their condition by telling Officer P that they have colds or headaches. Furthermore, aspirin is not medicine.

The CORRECT answer is:

A. I, III B. I, II C. III, IV
D. I, IV E. III, V

18. List the five BASIC principles of supervising prisoners on sick call and during their medical care. 18.____

1. ____________________
2. ____________________
3. ____________________
4. ____________________
5. ____________________

19. Supervising visiting is a dull assignment to Officer K. He manages to pass the time by concentrating on the visiting couple who are seated nearest him. Usually, he overhears some interesting conversations. Visiting in this jail is done in a room with tables that have a four-inch partition running through their center. Today, Officer K became so interested in the visit of the prisoner and his girlfriend seated near him that he didn't realize that he was permitting them and other prisoners to visit longer than regulations allowed. 19.____
Do you think Officer K has made any errors?

I. No; he was giving close supervision to the visitors.
II. Yes; it is not his responsibility to eavesdrop on visitors' conversations.
III. No; permitting visiting to last longer than regulations allow is not an error.
IV. Yes; he was distracted by one visitor and did not pay any attention to other visiting taking place.

The CORRECT answer is:

A. III, IV
B. III, V
C. II, IV
D. I, II
E. II, III

20. Which of the following descriptive statements are included in a definition of a trusty. A trusty 20.____

A. is a prisoner who can be trusted to work without supervision
B. is a prisoner who can work under minimum supervision
C. can be depended on not to escape
D. is a prisoner who because he can be trusted can be given responsibility to supervise the work of other prisoners and lock and unlock cells. He thus makes the work of jail personnel much easier.

21. What *special* privileges should trusties have that are NOT permitted to other prisoners? 21.____

A. Freedom to move about in the jail without special permission
B. Extra food because they work
C. Permitted to run errands for jail personnel
D. They should not have any special privileges

22. A prisoner being considered for trusty status should be evaluated in three areas. Indicate by writing in the kinds of information that should be examined. (List three kinds.) 22.____

1. ____________________
2. ____________________
3. ____________________

23. Why must juveniles be kept separate from adult prisoners? (List two reasons.) 23.____

1. ____________________
2. ____________________

24. In what way is supervision of women DIFFERENT from supervision for men? 24.____

____
____
____
____

25. Officer W has been supervising the recreation periods recently. Yesterday, he overruled the umpire's decision even though there had been no argument from either team. There was little doubt that the umpire had made a bad call. Today, he took part in a volleyball game in order to even sides. 25.____
Do you feel Officer W has made any errors?

A. *No;* he is correcting the umpire and thus avoiding complaints or arguments from prisoners.
B. *Yes;* it seems that the prisoner did not contest the call.
C. *Yes;* he is becoming involved with prisoner recreation activities when there is no need to do so, and he is ignoring his supervisory responsibility.
D. *No;* a supervisor should be alert to possible problems and try and solve them before they become serious. Correcting the umpire was correct. He is also contributing to the recreation period by participating in the game.

26. List the BASIC principles of supervising a prisoner at a funeral or other social activity outside the jail. (List three.) 26.____

1. ____________________
2. ____________________
3. ____________________

KEY (CORRECT ANSWERS)

1. D
2. C
3. D
4. Poor directions - too general; did not take into account the possibility that some of the prisoners may not have understood his orders; is not making periodic cheeks.
5. C
6. B, E
7. A. Discussed his off-duty activities with prisoners.
   B. Discussed his relationship with his wife with prisoners.
   C. Mention of the bowling score was not important, but this was an opening for the prisoners to make an insulting remark.
8. C
9. C
10. B
11. B
12. C
13. B
14. E
15. D
16. A. Deliver food while it is hot
    B. Supervisor must accompany the prisoner who is serving food
    C. Count utensils to and from prisoners
    D. Make seconds available as a means of preventing stronger prisoners from stealing food from the weak.
17. A
18. A. Do not diagnose.
    B. Supervise prisoners closely when they are taking medication.
    C. Never give out more than one dose of medication at one time.
    D. Keep accurate medical records.
    E. Permit all prisoners' sick call requests.
19. C
20. B
21. D
22. A. Escape record and detainers
    B. Work habits
    C. Behavior in confinement
23. A. To prevent adults from possibly sexually assaulting them.
    B. To keep juveniles from being exposed to hardened criminal types
24. There is no basic difference. The same principles and techniques can be used. Women must be kept separate from male prisoners.
25. C
26. A. Do not remove cuffs unless prior approval has been given by the jail administrator.
    B. Keep the prisoner in sight at all times.
    C. No special visits or other requests to be granted.

TEST 5

DIRECTIONS: Each question or incomplete statement is followed by several suggested answers or completions. Select the one that BEST answers the question or completes the statement. *PRINT THE LETTER OF THE CORRECT ANSWER IN THE SPACE AT THE RIGHT.*

1. The GOAL of discipline in jail is to 1.___

   A. teach prisoners absolute obedience to orders
   B. teach acceptable behavior
   C. teach prisoners self-control
   D. control prisoners

2. Written rules serve the following purposes: 2.___
   I. To inform prisoners what not to do
   II. To inform prisoners about what is expected of them
   III. To establish standards for evaluating prisoners' conduct
   IV. Take authority away from jail officers who should be responsible for establishing standards of conduct

   The CORRECT answer is:

   A. I, II B. I, III C. II, IV
   D. III, IV E. II, III

3. Officer O has a temper that he displays whenever a prisoner gets on his nerves. He insists that prisoners do what they are told and that they follow the rules to the letter. It is his opinion that generally people get into trouble with the law because they lack discipline. He feels that it is his responsibility to teach prisoners discipline. 3.___
   Do you feel that Officer O is CORRECT?

   A. *Yes;* prisoners will generally take advantage of an officer who is not very strict.
   B. *No;* Officer O is too strict. He probably antagonizes prisoners by his attitude.
   C. *Yes;* all jail officers have a responsibility to teach prisoners discipline.
   D. *Yes;* however, he certainly sets a poor example by his display of temper.

4. Officer A caught two prisoners horsing around and decided to punish them by making them run in place. He reasoned that this would tire them so that they would not have the energy for horseplay. 4.___
   Do you think his actions were PROPER?

   A. *Yes;* prisoners learn a lesson from immediate punishment.
   B. *No;* the officer who sees the infraction should not, as a rule, also decide the punishment.
   C. Both of the above
   D. None of the above

5. Officer S is a firm believer in keeping order. He practices this belief and, as a result, turns in a high number of disciplinary reports. 5.___
   Do you think that S is acting properly?

   A. *Yes;* all infractions of rules should be reported.
   B. *No;* he should only report infractions that are serious and that cannot be handled informally.
   C. Both of the above
   D. None of the above

6. The following is a list of rule violations. Indicate those that require formal action and those that may be handled informally. (Use letter F for formal and letter I for informal.) 6.

   A. Loud and continuous noise A.____
   B. Talking after lights out B.____
   C. Horseplay in sick call line C.____
   D. Arguing with waiter in serving line D.____
   E. Evidence of bar tampering E.____
   F. Contraband (knife) F.____
   G. Contraband (money) G.____
   H. Contraband (book) H.____
   I. Holding up line when returning to cells I.____

7. Officer D has taken Prisoner E out of line for horseplay and is correcting him before a group of interested prisoners. What do you think are the possible consequences of this action? 7.____

   A. Prisoner E will learn a lesson.
   B. Prisoner E may become angry at being embarrassed in front of other prisoners.
   C. Officer D has realized that this was an excellent opportunity to teach E proper behavior and will make a positive impression on the prisoner.
   D. The other prisoners will also have an opportunity to learn from Prisoner E's experience.

8. Prisoner O became abusive toward another prisoner, and they were on the edge of fighting when Officer C arrived on the scene. Both prisoners continued to argue, and a shoving contest began. 8.____
   What should Officer C do?

   A. Step between the prisoners and separate them.
   B. Grab Prisoner O and pull him away.
   C. Shout to both prisoners to stop.
   D. He had better call another officer for assistance and then step in.

9. Officer S is a large man and quite sure of himself. Today, when Prisoner N refused to come out of his cell to take a shower, Officer S went in and took him out. 9.____
   Do you think this was the proper method?

   A. *Yes;* prisoners should do what they are told.
   B. *No;* the prisoner should have been permitted to remain in his cell until he decided to come out.
   C. *Yes;* prisoners must conform to all schedules.
   D. If it was necessary that Prisoner N come out of his cell, the officer should not have gone in alone to take him out.

10. Prisoner N has declared that he is on a hunger strike and has refused to eat three meals in a row. A number of officers are upset by N's behavior and feel that something should be done about him. 10.____
Which do you feel is the PROPER procedure?

A. Force feed him; all prisoners should eat three meals a day.
B. Ignore him; he will eat when he is hungry.
C. Wait a few days; and if he continues to refuse food, he should be force fed.
D. Refer him to the doctor who can make a decision if and when he will require any medical care and forced feeding.

KEY (CORRECT ANSWERS)

1. C
2. E
3. D
4. B
5. B
6. Formal: E, F, G, H
   Informal: A, B, C, D
7. B
8. D
9. D
10. D

TEST 6

DIRECTIONS: Each question or incomplete statement is followed by several suggested answers or completions. Select the one that BEST answers the question or completes the statement. *PRINT THE LETTER OF THE CORRECT ANSWER IN THE SPACE AT THE RIGHT.*

1. A prisoner is brought to the jail with the following symptoms: shakiness, staggering, thick speech, and a blank glassy-eyed look. 1.____
   Select the PROPER action to be taken.

   A. He is drunk; place him in the drunk tank.
   B. Although he may be drunk, it is possible that he may have a serious injury or illness. He should be referred to a doctor.
   C. Both of the above
   D. None of the above

2. Shortly after being admitted, a prisoner begins to shake, does not talk clearly, and claims to see bugs crawling over him. 2.____
   The jailer should do one of the following:

   A. The prisoner is obviously psychotic and should be referred to the doctor
   B. The prisoner is having *DTs;* the doctor should be called immediately
   C. Although the prisoner is acting strangely, he should be observed for a time until it is obvious that he is sick
   D. None of the above

3. Prisoner E has been in jail two weeks waiting trial. Lately, he has been acting strangely. He has been talking to an imaginary person, laughing and arguing. Today he accused Officer T of trying to *get him.* 3.____
   What should the officer do?

   A. Observe Prisoner E and submit a report to the administrator for medical referral
   B. Warn E to quiet down because he is disturbing others
   C. Try to prove to Prisoner E that the officer is not trying to get him
   D. None of the above

4. Prisoner L seems to have a habit of talking to himself, especially when he is playing solitaire. During the last week, he has also been complaining about his physical condition, claiming that he has a bad heart and that he is afraid it will stop one of these days soon. 4.____
   What should the officer do?

   A. It seems that L is becoming psychotic; he should be referred to the doctor.
   B. L's talking to himself is not a symptom of psychosis, but his physical complaint is; write a report and refer him to the doctor.
   C. There is nothing wrong with L; and since he has not requested medical attention, he should be left alone.
   D. Write a report on his complaints and refer him to the doctor. He may not be psychotic, but his medical complaint should be referred.

5. Prisoner V is charged with petty theft. Apparently, he absent-mindedly walked out of a store with a pair of gloves. Now he claims that he is innocent because he had money to pay for the gloves. Furthermore, he says that he has a bank account with ten thousand dollars. The other prisoners laugh at him, which only makes him angry. Since he has no money and no family, he has not called anyone. Now he wants an attorney and wants to call the largest bank in town for a release of funds. 5.____
What should the officer do?

   A. It is obvious that V is senile. He demonstrated this by forgetting he had the gloves when he left the store. Refer to the doctor.
   B. V is hallucinating; he certainly does not behave as though he has money. Refuse him permission to call the bank and refer to the doctor.
   C. Have V give his account number or other method of identifying himself and call the bank. If he has no account, refer to the doctor.
   D. None of the above

6. Officer Y has been watching Prisoner O for the last few days because he felt that O was acting strange. He finally sent a referral memo to the jail administrator that contained the following information: *Prisoner O has been acting strangely the last few days. He seems frightened, mumbles to himself, and walks the floor of his cell a lot. I think he should be seen by the doctor.* 6.____
Do you think this report contains sufficient information?

   A. *Yes;* it tells the doctor that the prisoner is acting strangely.
   B. *No;* there is not enough information.
   C. *Yes;* even though there is little information, there is enough for a doctor to know that something is wrong with the prisoner.
   D. *No;* there is very little description. It does not describe how the prisoner acts when frightened, how much walking is a lot, or contain any information that might show if the prisoner is talking to himself or hallucinating.

7. Prisoner G is very forgetful; he can't remember simple rules or follow instructions too well. He is a disciplinary problem because he always seems to be involved in some kind of illegal activity. Yesterday, he was caught with a knife. He claimed he was only carrying it for Prisoner B and claimed he did not know it is contraband. G is a youthful appearing 25 years. 7.____
What action should be taken?

   A. G is suffering from extreme advanced senility; refer him for a medical exam.
   B. G is a good liar and is only trying to get out of trouble now that he has been caught.
   C. G seems to be mentally deficient. Rather than harsh punishment, he needs to have someone explain rules to him more clearly. He also needs closer supervision.
   D. None of the above

8. Prisoner J appeared normal when he was admitted to the jail two days ago. Now he seems to be ill. He complains of aching muscles, is weak, and has lost his appetite, and is vomiting. 8.____
What seems to be his problem and what should the officer do?

   A. Sounds like flu; refer to the doctor.
   B. J is having drug withdrawal symptoms. He should be referred to the doctor, kept isolated from others, and closely supervised.
   C. J is suffering from insulin shock. He should be kept in a cell away from others until he calms down in a few days.
   D. Sounds like nothing. None of the above.

9. A person on drug withdrawal requires special care, including isolation and close supervision because 9.____

A. drug addicts are usually dangerous and should always be housed in maximum security conditions
B. he needs to be closely supervised to keep him away from drugs
C. to prevent him from bothering others, to make it easier to control him, provide close supervision in case he attempts to injure himself
D. all of the above

10. Officer D has on a number of occasions referred to *sex fiends* and how it is necessary to exercise care when around them because they are dangerous. 10.____
Do you agree?

A. *Yes;* it is not possible to predict just what a sex offender will do.
B. *No;* sex offenders are not dangerous while in jail, but I wouldn't want to meet one on the street.
C. *Yes;* anyone who would commit sex crimes must be untrustworthy and dangerous.
D. *No;* there are all types of sex offenders, and only a few are violent or dangerous.

11. Officer H has worked in the jail for many years. He is rightfully proud of his ability and experience. He claims that he can always spot a homosexual by his walk and feminine behavior. 11.____
Do you think that Officer H is CORRECT?

A. *Yes;* all hmosexuals walk like girls and act feminine.
B. *No;* it is not possible to identify a homosexual without interviewing him.
C. *Yes;* it's very simple. They are usually slim and have delicate features.
D. *No;* some masculine-appearing men are homosexual, and often slim delicately-built men are not. It is not appearance but behavior that must be examined.

12. Prisoner Y is slim and has a limp-wristed feminine appearance. Prisoner W is husky and aggressive. Y pretty much minds his own business and does his time. W is loud and is trying very hard to become friends with Y. He keeps offering Y cigarettes and candy which Y refuses. What do you suspect is happening? 12.____

A. Nothing; W is just trying to be friendly.
B. Obviously Y is homosexual and W doesn't seem to realize it.
C. Y may or may not be a homosexual; his behavior so far does not indicate that he is. W, however, is acting like an aggressive homosexual and trying to get close to Y.
D. None of the above

13. Indicate whether the following statements are TRUE or FALSE: 13.

A. Homosexuals can be easily identified. A.____
B. A person who talks to himself is psychotic. B.____
C. People who threaten suicide will not attempt it. C.____
D. People who threaten suicide are just trying to get sympathy. D.____
E. Young people have a high suicide rate. E.____
F. The best method of handling a person who threatens suicide is to call his bluff. F.____
G. Keeping suicide risks isolated from others is the best way to manage them G.____

14. Prisoner K appears sick. His face is flushed, his skin is dry, and his mouth is dry. His breath is noticeably sweet. 14.___
What should you do?

A. Give him some aspirin and permit him to go on sick call.
B. Give him orange juice or something else with sugar in it because he is having insulin shock.
C. Call the doctor immediately; he is suffering from inadequate insulin.
D. Ignore the matter.

15. Prisoner P complains of not feeling well. He is pale and weak, his skin is moist, and he seems to be quite shaky as though he were intoxicated. P claims he is diabetic and is in need of something with sugar in it to correct this condition. 15.___
What would you do?

A. Check the records and, if they show he is diabetic, call the doctor and ask for instructions.
B. Ignore him because this is just another way for some prisoners to get something extra to eat.
C. Give him candy or orange juice; he is showing symptoms of insulin shock. If he does not feel better almost at once, call the doctor.
D. Give him the back of your hand.

16. Prisoner J is having a seizure in his cell. 16.___
What should the officer do? (Select five.)

A. Hold him down so that he does not injure himself.
B. Remove nearby objects so that he does not injure himself.
C. Sit him up and give him water to drink.
D. Wait until the seizure is over and then give him his medication.
E. Loosen clothing around neck and place a padded object between his teeth to prevent his biting his tongue.
F. Place coat or pillow beneath prisoner's head to prevent injury.
G. Turn his face to one side.
H. Notify the doctor immediately.
I. The doctor should be routinely informed.

17. Prisoner J has had four seizures in the last hour. You have followed the proper procedure in helping him in each instance. 17.___
What do you do NEXT?

A. Make certain that he is taking his medication.
B. Restrain him on his bed so that he does not injure himself during the next seizure.
C. Call the doctor immediately in order to provide emergency care.
D. All of the above

18. As a result of a seizure, Prisoner J has received a head injury. The wound located above the right ear is bleeding. In addition, there seems to be watery fluid flowing from his nose. His breathing is slow and difficult. As yet, he has not regained consciousness as he usually does immediately after a seizure. 18.____
What should you do?

A. Let him sleep; he must be tired from the seizure.
B. Apply a pressure bandage to stop the bleeding.
C. Call the doctor; there seems to be evidence that he may have a serious head wound.
D. Call the warden.
E. Nothing; he's trying to divert your attention.

19. The jail officer's responsibility in managing special prisoners includes the following areas: (Select four.) 19.____

A. Diagnosing prisoners' physical and mental condition and referring to the doctor.
B. Giving first aid whenever it is needed.
C. Noticing strange or unusual behavior and referring to the doctor.
D. Developing the ability to describe the physical and emotional condition of prisoners objectively.
E. Prepare records that describe prisoners' injuries and record their medical complaints.
F. Evaluate prisoner medical complaints, prescribe medication when required, and keep the chronic complainers from sick call.
G. Closely supervise the taking of medication, keep careful records of all medicine distributed to and taken by prisoners.

KEY (CORRECT ANSWERS)

1. B
2. B
3. A
4. D
5. C

6. D
7. C
8. B
9. C
10. D

11. D
12. C
13. A. F
    B. F
    C. F
    D. F
    E. T
    F. F
    G. F
14. C
15. C

16. B, E, F, G, I
17. C
18. C
19. C, D, E, G

EXAMINATION SECTION
TEST 1

DIRECTIONS: Each question or incomplete statement is followed by several suggested answers or completions. Select the one that BEST answers the question or completes the statement. *PRINT THE LETTER OF THE CORRECT ANSWER IN THE SPACE AT THE RIGHT.*

Questions 1-6.

DIRECTIONS: Questions 1 through 6 are to be answered on the basis of the following list of items permitted in cells.

ITEMS PERMITTED IN CELLS	
comb	mop
spoon	towel
cup	letters
envelopes	pen
broom	soap
washcloth	money
writing paper	chair
books	dustpan
toothpaste	brushes
toothbrush	pencil

The questions consist of sets of pictures of four objects labeled A, B, C, and D. Choose the one object that is NOT in the above list of items permitted and mark its letter in the space at the right. Disregard any information you may have about what is or is not permitted in any institution. Base your answers SOLELY on the above list. Mark only one answer for each question.

1. 1.____

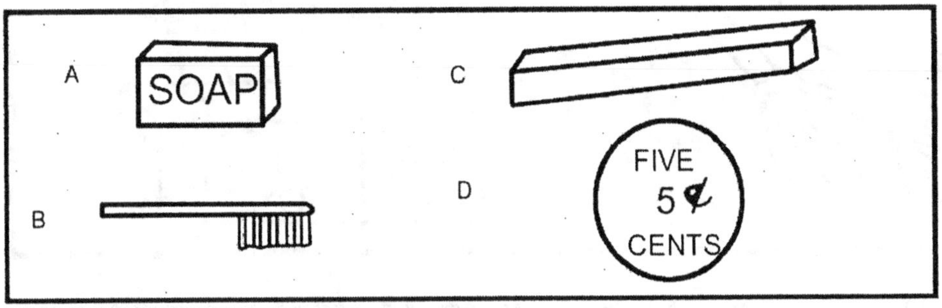

2. 2.____

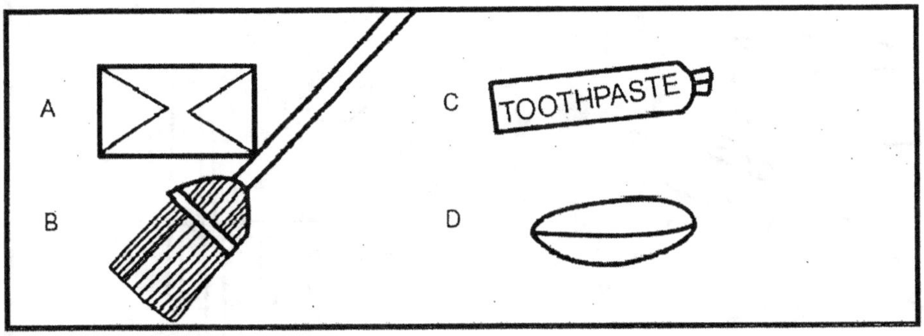

3.

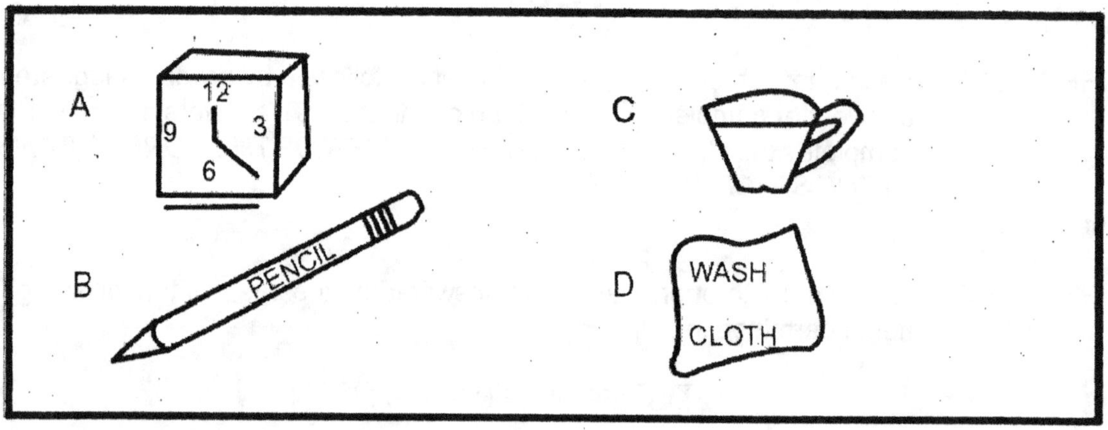

3.____

4.

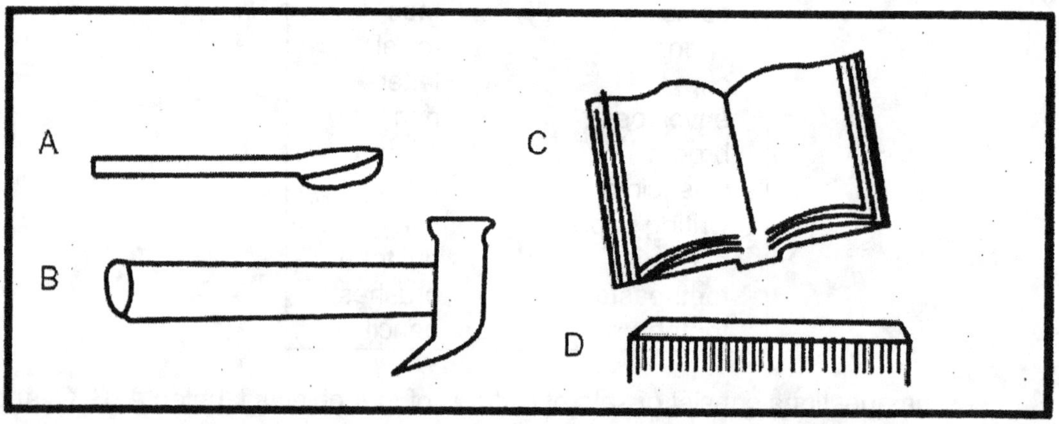

4.____

5.

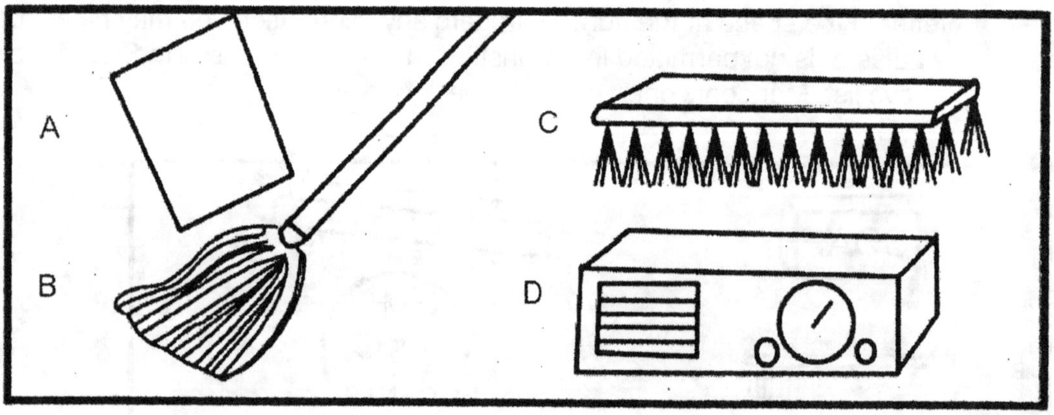

5.____

6.

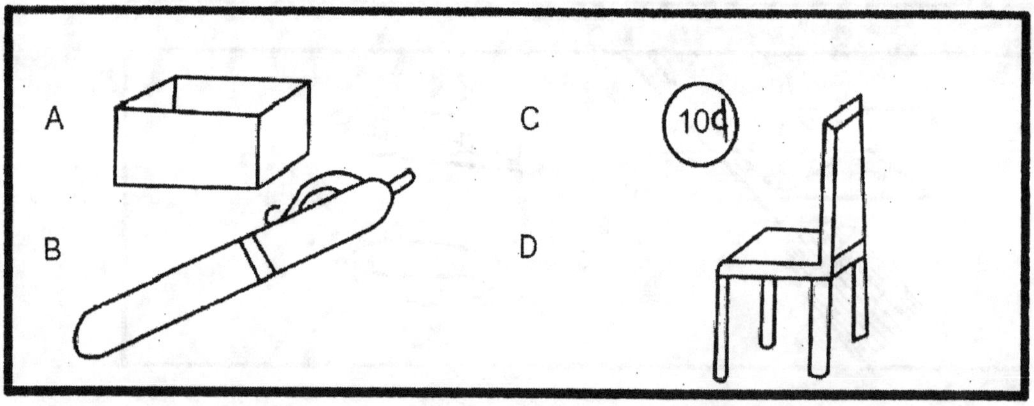

6.____

Questions 7-11.

DIRECTIONS: Questions 7 through 11 are to be answered on the basis of the following list showing the name and number of each of nine inmates.

1	- Johnson	4	- Thompson	7	- Gordon
2	- Smith	5	- Frank	8	- Porter
3	- Edwards	6	- Murray	9	- Lopez

Each question consists of 3 sets of numbers and letters.
Each set should consist of the numbers of three inmates and the first letter of each of their names. The letters should be in the same order as the numbers. In at least two of the three choices, there will be an error.

In the space at the right, mark only that choice in which the letters correspond with the numbers and are in the same order. If all three sets are wrong, mark Choice D in the space at the right.

SAMPLE QUESTION: A. 386 EPM
B. 542 FST
C. 474 LGT

Since 3 corresponds to E for Edwards, 8 corresponds to P for Porter, and 6 corresponds to M for Murray, Choice A is correct and should be entered in the answer space. Choice B is wrong because letters T and S have been reversed. Choice C is wrong because the first number, which is 4, does NOT correspond with the first letter of Choice C, which is L. It should have been T. If Choice A were also wrong, then D would have been the correct answer.

7. A. 382 EGS B. 461 TMJ C. 875 PLF 7.____

8. A. 549 FLT B. 692 MJS C. 758 GSP 8.____

9. A. 936 LEM B. 253 FSE C. 147 JTL 9.____

10. A. 569 PML B. 716 GJP C. 842 PTS 10.____

11. A. 356 FEM B. 198 JPL C. 637 MEG 11.____

Questions 12-16.

DIRECTIONS: Questions 12 through 16 are to be answered on the basis of the following passage.

Mental disorders are found in a fairly large number of the inmates in correctional institutions. There are no exact figures as to the number of inmates who are mentally disturbed—partly because it is hard to draw a precise line between "mental disturbance" and "normality"—but experts find that somewhere between 15% and 25% of inmates are suffering from disorders that are obvious enough to show up in routine psychiatric examinations. Society has not yet really come to grips with the problem of what to do with mentally disturbed offenders. There is not enough money available to set up treatment programs for all the people identified as mentally disturbed; and there would probably not be enough qualified psychiatric personnel available to run such programs even if they could be set up. Most mentally disturbed offenders are therefore left to serve out their time in correctional institutions, and the burden of dealing with them falls on correction officers. This means that a correction officer must be sensitive enough to human behavior to know when he is dealing with a person who is not mentally normal, and that the officer must be imaginative enough to be able to sense how an abnormal individual might react under certain circumstances.

12. According to the above passage, mentally disturbed inmates in correctional institutions 12.____

   A. are usually transferred to mental hospitals when their condition is noticed
   B. cannot be told from other inmates because tests cannot distinguish between insane people and normal people
   C. may constitute as much as 25% of the total inmate population
   D. should be regarded as no different from all the other inmates

13. The above passage says that today the job of handling mentally disturbed inmates is MAINLY up to 13.____

   A. psychiatric personnel
   B. other inmates
   C. correction officers
   D. administrative officials

14. Of the following, which is a reason given in the above passage for society's failure to provide adequate treatment programs for mentally disturbed inmates? 14.____

   A. Law-abiding citizens should not have to pay for fancy treatment programs for citizens.
   B. A person who breaks the law should not expect society to give him special help.
   C. It is impossible to tell whether an inmate is mentally disturbed.
   D. There are not enough trained people to provide the kind of treatment needed.

15. The expression *abnormal individual,* as used in the last sentence of the above passage, refers to an individual who is 15.____

   A. of average intelligence
   B. of superior intelligence
   C. completely normal
   D. mentally disturbed

16. The reader of the above passage would MOST likely agree that 16.____

   A. correction officers should not expect mentally disturbed persons to behave the same way a normal person would behave
   B. correction officers should not report infractions
   C. of the rules committed by mentally disturbed persons
   D. mentally disturbed persons who break the law should be treated exactly the same way as anyone else
   E. mentally disturbed persons who have broken the law should not be imprisoned

Questions 17-23.

DIRECTIONS: Questions 17 through 23 are to be answered on the basis of the roster of inmates, the instructions, the table, and the sample question given below.

Twelve inmates of a correctional institution are divided into three permanent groups in their workshop. They must be present and accounted for in these groups at the beginning of each workday. During the day, the inmates check out of their groups for various activities.

They check back in again when those activities have been completed. Assume that the day is divided into three activity periods.

ROSTER OF INMATES

GROUP X	Ted	Frank	George	Harry
GROUP Y	Jack	Ken	Larry	Mel
GROUP Z	Phil	Bob	Sam	Vic

The following table shows the movements of these inmates from their groups during the day. Assume that all were present and accounted for at the beginning of Period I.

		GROUP X	GROUP Y	GROUP Z
Period I	Check-outs	Ted, Frank	Ken, Larry	Phil
Period II	Check- ins	Frank	Ken, Larry	Phil
	Check-outs	George	Jack, Mel	Bob, Sam, Vic
Period III	Check-ins	George	Mel, Jack	Sam, Bob, Vic
	Check-outs	Frank, Harry	Ken	Vic

SAMPLE QUESTION: At the end of Period II, the inmates remaining in Group X were

A. Ted, Frank, Harry
B. Frank, Harry
C. Ted, George
D. Frank, Harry, George

During Period I, Ted and Frank were checked out from Group X. During Period II, Frank was checked back in, and George was checked out. Therefore, the members of the group remaining out are Ted and George. The two other members of the group, Frank and Harry, should be present. The correct answer is B.

17. At the end of Period I, the TOTAL number of inmates remaining in their own permanent groups was 17._____

A. 8 B. 7 C. 6 D. 5

18. At the end of Period I, the inmates remaining in Group Z were 18._____

A. George and Harry
B. Jack and Mel
C. Bob, Sam, and Vic
D. Phil

19. At the end of Period II, the inmates remaining in Group Y were 19._____

A. Ken and Larry
B. Jack, Ken, and Mel
C. Jack and Ken
D. Ken, Mel, and Larry

20. At the end of Period II, the TOTAL number of inmates remaining in their own permanent groups was 20._____

A. 8 B. 7 C. 6 D. 5

21. At the end of Period II, the inmates who were NOT present in Group Z were 21._____

A. Phil, Bob, and Sam
B. Sam, Bob, and Vic
C. Sam, Vic, and Phil
D. Vic, Phil, and Bob

22. At the end of Period III, the inmates remaining in Group Y were 22.___

A. Ted, Frank, and George
B. Jack, Mel, and Ken
C. Jack, Larry, and Mel
D. Frank and Harry

23. At the end of Period III, the TOTAL number of inmates NOT present in their own permanent groups was 23.___

A. 4 B. 5 C. 6 D. 7

24. Of the 100 inmates in a certain cellblock, one-half were assigned to clean-up work, and one-fifth were assigned to work in the laundry. 24.___
How many inmates were NOT assigned for clean-up work or laundry work?

A. 30 B. 40 C. 50 D. 60

25. A certain cellblock has a maximum capacity of 250 inmates. On March 26, there were 200 inmates housed in the cellblock. 12 inmates were added on that day, and 17 inmates were added on the following day. No inmates left on either day. 25.___
How many more inmates could this cellblock have accommodated on the second day?

A. 11 B. 16 C. 21 D. 28

KEY (CORRECT ANSWERS)

1. C
2. D
3. A
4. B
5. D

6. A
7. B
8. D
9. A
10. C

11. C
12. C
13. C
14. D
15. D

16. A
17. B
18. C
19. A
20. D

21. B
22. C
23. B
24. A
25. C

TEST 2

DIRECTIONS: Each question or incomplete statement is followed by several suggested answers or completions. Select the one that BEST answers the question or completes the statement. *PRINT THE LETTER OF THE CORRECT ANSWER IN THE SPACE AT THE RIGHT.*

Questions 1-5.

DIRECTIONS: Questions 1 through 5 are to be answered SOLELY on the basis of the Report of Offense that appears below.

REPORT OF OFFENSE		Report No.	*26743*
		Date of Report	*10-12*
Inmate	*Joseph Brown*		
Age	*27*	Number	*61274*
Sentence	*90 days*	Assignment	*KU-187*
Place of Offense	*R.P.W. 4-1*	Date of Offense	*10/11*
Offense	*Assaulting inmate*		
Details	*During 9:00 p.m. cellblock clean-up, inmate John Jones asked for pail being used by Brown. Brown refused. Correction officer requested that Brown comply. Brown then threw pail at Jones with intent to injure him and said he would "get" Jones. Jones not hurt.*		
Force Used by Officer	*None*		
Name of Reporting Officer	*R. Rodriguez*	No.	*C-2056*
Name of Superior Officer	*P. Ferguson*		

1. The person who made out this report is 1.____

   A. Joseph Brown
   B. John Jones
   C. R. Rodriguez
   D. P. Ferguson

2. Disregarding the details, the specific offense reported was 2.____

   A. insulting a fellow inmate
   B. assaulting a fellow inmate
   C. injuring a fellow inmate
   D. disobeying a correction officer

3. The number of the inmate who committed the offense is 3.____

   A. 26743
   B. 61274
   C. KU-187
   D. C-2056

4. The offense took place on 4.____

   A. October 11
   B. June 12
   C. December
   D. November 13

5. The place where the offense occurred is identified in the report as 5.____

   A. Brown's cell
   B. Jones' cell
   C. KU-187
   D. R.P.W., 4-1

6. Add $51.79, $29.39, and $8.98. 6.____
The CORRECT answer is

A. $78.97 B. $88.96 C. $89.06 D. $90.16

7. Add $72.07 and $31.54, then subtract $25.75. 7.____
The CORRECT answer is

A. $77.86 B. $82.14 C. $88.96 D. $129.36

8. Start with $82.47, then subtract $25.50, $4.75, and 35¢. 8.____
The CORRECT answer is

A. $30.60 B. $51.87 C. $52.22 D. $65.25

9. Add $19.35 and $37.75, then subtract $9.90 and $19.80. 9.____
The CORRECT answer is

A. $27.40 B. $37.00 C. $37.30 D. $47.20

10. Multiply $38.85 by 2; then subtract $27.90. 10.____
The CORRECT answer is

A. $21.90 B. $48.70 C. $49.80 D. $50.70

11. Add $53.66, $9.27, and $18.75, then divide by 2. 11.____
The CORRECT answer is

A. $35.84 B. $40.34 C. $40.84 D. $41.34

12. Out of 192 inmates in a certain cellblock, 96 are to go on a work detail and another 32 are to report to a vocational class. All the rest are to remain in the cellblock. 12.____
How many inmates should be left on the cellblock?

A. 48 B. 64 C. 86 D. 128

13. Assume that you, as a correction officer, are responsible for seeing that the right number of utensils are counted out for a meal. You need enough utensils for 620 men. One fork and one spoon are needed for each man. In addition, one ladle is needed for each group of 20 men. 13.____
How many utensils will be needed altogether?

A. 1240 B. 1271 C. 1550 D. 1860

14. Assume that you, as a correction officer, are supervising the inmates who are assigned to a dishwashing detail. There is a direct relationship between the amount of time it takes to do all the dishwashing and the number of inmates who are washing dishes. When two inmates are washing dishes, the job takes six hours. 14.____
If there are four inmates washing dishes, how long should the job take?
_______ hour(s).

A. 1 B. 2 C. 3 D. 4

15. Assume that you, as a correction officer, are in charge of supervising the laundry sorting and counting. You expect that on a certain day there will be nearly 7,000 items to be sorted and counted. 15.____
If one inmate can sort and count 500 items in an hour, how many inmates are needed to sort all 7,000 items in one hour?

A. 2 B. 5 C. 7 D. 14

16. A carpentry course is being given for inmates who want to learn a skill. The course will be taught in several different groups. Each group should contain at least 12 but not more than 16 men. The smaller the group, the better, as long as there are at least 12 men per group. If 66 inmates are going to take the course, they should be divided into 16.____

A. 4 groups of 16 men
B. 4 groups of 13 men and 1 group of 14 men
C. 3 groups of 13 men and 2 groups of 14 men
D. 6 groups of 11 men

Questions 17-21.

DIRECTIONS: Questions 17 through 21 are to be answered on the basis of the Fact Situation and the Report of Inmate Injury form below. The questions ask how the report form should be filled in, based on the information given in the Fact Situation.

FACT SITUATION

Peter Miller is a correction officer assigned to duty in Cellblock A. His superior officer is John Doakes. Miller was on duty at 1:30 P.M. on March 21, 2004, when he heard a scream for help from Cell 12. He hurried to Cell 12 and found inmate Richard Rogers stamping out a flaming book of matches. Inmate John Jones was screaming. It seems that Jones had accidentally set fire to the entire book of matches while lighting a cigarette, and he had burned his left hand. Smoking was permitted at this hour. Miller reported the incident by phone, and Jones was escorted to the dispensary where his hand was treated at 2:00 P.M. by Dr. Albert Lorillo. Dr. Lorillo determined that Jones could return to his cellblock, but that he should be released from work for four days. The doctor scheduled a re-examination for March 22. A routine investigation of the incident was made by James Lopez. Jones confirmed to this officer that the above statement of the situation was correct.

REPORT OF INMATE INJURY

(1) Name of Inmate ______ (2) Assignment ______
(3) Number ______ (4) Location ______
(5) Nature of Injury ______ (6) Date ______
(7) Details (how, when, where injury was incurred) ______

(8) Received medical attention: Date ______ Time ______
(9) Treatment ______
(10) Disposition (check one or more):
___ (10-1) Return to housing area ___ (10-2) Return to duty
___ (10-3) Work release ___ ___ days ___ (10-4) Re-examine in ___ days

(11) Employing reporting injury ______
(12) Employee's supervisor or superior officer ______
(13) Medical officer treating injury ______
(14) Investigating officer ______
(15) Head of institution ______

17. Which of the following should be entered in Item 1? 17.___

A. Peter Miller B. John Doakes
C. Richard Rogers D. John Jones

18. Which of the following should be entered in Item 11? 18.___

A. Peter Miller B. James Lopez
C. Richard Rogers D. John Jones

19. Which of the following should be entered in Item 8? 19.___

A. 2/21/04, 1:30 P.M. B. 2/21/04, 2:00 P.M.
C. 3/21/04, 1:30 P.M. D. 3/21/04, 2:00 P.M.

20. For Item 10, which of the following should be checked? 20.___

A. Only 10-4 B. 10-1 and 10-4
C. 10-1, 10-3, and 10-4 D. 10-2, 10-3, and 10-4

21. Of the following items, which one CANNOT be filled in on the basis of the information given in the Fact Situation? 21.___
Item ______.

A. 12 B. 13 C. 14 D. 15

Questions 22-25.

DIRECTIONS: Questions 22 through 25 are to be answered on the basis of the chart which appears on the following page. The chart shows an 8-hour schedule for 4 groups of inmates. The numbers across the top of the chart stand for hours of the day: the hour beginning at 8:00, the hour beginning at 9:00, and so forth. The exact number of men in each group is given at the lefthand side of the chart. An hour when the men in a particular group are scheduled to be OUT of their cellblock is marked with an X.

	8	9	10	11	12	1	2	3
GROUP Q 44 men	X		X			X		
GROUP R 60 men	X		X	X		X	X	
GROUP S 24 men	X				X			
GROUP T 28 men	X		X		X			

22. How many of the men were in their cellblock from 11:00 to 12:00? 22.____

    A. 60 B. 96 C. 104 D. 156

23. At 10:45, how many of the men were NOT in their cellblock? 23.____

    A. 24 B. 60 C. 96 D. 132

24. At 12:30, what proportion of the men were NOT in their cellblock? 24.____

    A. 1/4 B. 1/3 C. 1/2 D. 2/3

25. During the period covered in the chart, what percentage of the time did the men in Group S spend in their cellblock? 25.____

    A. 60% B. 65% C. 70% D. 75%

KEY (CORRECT ANSWERS)

1. C
2. B
3. B
4. A
5. D
6. D
7. A
8. B
9. A
10. C
11. C
12. B
13. B
14. C
15. D
16. B
17. D
18. A
19. D
20. C
21. D
22. B
23. D
24. B
25. D

EXAMINATION SECTION
TEST 1

DIRECTIONS: Each question or incomplete statement is followed by several suggested answers or completions. Select the one that BEST answers the question or completes the statement. *PRINT THE LETTER OF THE CORRECT ANSWER IN THE SPACE AT THE RIGHT.*

Questions 1-25.

DIRECTIONS: Questions 1 through 25 describe situations which might occur in a correctional institution. The institution houses its inmates in cells divided into groups called cellblocks. In answering the questions, assume that you are a correction officer.

1. *Correction officers are often required to search inmates and the various areas of the correctional institution for any items which may be considered dangerous or which are not permitted. In making a routine search, officers should not neglect to examine an item just because it is usually regarded as a permitted item. For instance, some innocent-looking object can be converted into a weapon by sharpening one of its parts or replacing a part with a sharpened or pointed blade.* 1.____

   Which of the following objects could MOST easily be converted into a weapon in this way? A

   A. ballpoint pen
   B. pad of paper
   C. crayon
   D. handkerchief

2. *Only authorized employees are permitted to handle keys. Under no circumstances should an inmate be permitted to use door keys. When not in use, all keys are to be deposited with the security officer.* 2.____

   Which one of the following actions does NOT violate these regulations?

   A. A correction officer has given a trusted inmate the key to a supply room and sends the inmate to bring back a specific item from that room.
   B. A priest comes to make authorized visits to inmates. The correction officer is very busy, so he gives the priest the keys needed to reach certain groups of cells.
   C. An inmate has a pass to go to the library. A cellblock officer examines the pass, then unlocks the door and lets the inmate through.
   D. At the end of the day, a correction officer puts his keys in the pocket of his street clothes and takes them home with him.

3. *Decisions about handcuffing or restraining inmates are often up to the correction officers involved. However, an officer is legally responsible for exercising good judgment and for taking necessary precautions to prevent harm both to the inmate involved and to others.* 3.____

   In which one of the following situations is handcuffing or other physical restraint MOST likely to be needed?

A. An inmate seems to have lost control of his senses and is banging his fists repeatedly against the bars of his cell.
B. During the past two weeks, an inmate has deliberately tried to start three fights with other inmates.
C. An inmate claims to be sick and refuses to leave his cell for a scheduled meal.
D. During the night, an inmate begins to shout and sing, disturbing the sleep of other inmates.

4. *Some utensils that are ordinarily used in a kitchen can also serve as dangerous weapons – for instance, vegetable parers, meat saws, skewers, and icepicks. These should be classified as extremely hazardous.* 4.___

The MOST sensible way of solving the problems caused by the use of these utensils in a correctional institution is to

A. try to run the kitchen without using any of these utensils
B. provide careful supervision of inmates using such utensils in the kitchen
C. assign only trusted inmates to kitchen duty and let them use the tools without regular supervision
D. take no special precautions since inmates are not likely to think of using these commonplace utensils as weapons

5. *Inmates may try to conceal objects that can be used as weapons or as escape devices. Therefore, routine searches of cells or dormitories are necessary for safety and security.* 5.___

Of the following, it would probably be MOST effective to schedule routine searches to take place

A. on regular days and always at the same time of day
B. on regular days but at different times of day
C. at frequent but irregular intervals, always at the same time of day
D. at frequent but irregular intervals and at different times of day

6. *One of the purposes of conducting routine searches for forbidden items is to discourage inmates from acquiring such items in the first place. Inmates should soon come to realize that only possessors of these items have reason to fear or resent such searches.* 6.___

Inmates are MOST likely to come to this realization if

A. the searching officer leaves every inmate's possessions in a mess to make it clear that a search has taken place
B. the searching officer confiscates something from every cell, though he may later return most of the items
C. other inmates are not told when a forbidden item is found in an inmate's possession
D. all inmates know that possession of a forbidden item will result in punishment

7. Suppose you are a correction officer supervising a work detail of 22 inmates. All 22 checked in at the start of the work period. Making an informal count an hour later, you count only 21 inmates. 7.___
What is the FIRST action to take?

A. Count again to make absolutely sure how many inmates are present.
B. Report immediately that an inmate has escaped.
C. Try to figure out where the missing inmate could be.
D. Wait until the end of the work period and then make a formal roll call.

8. *The officer who is making a count at night when inmates are in bed must make sure he sees each man. The rule "see living breathing flesh" must be followed in making accurate counts.* 8.____

Of the following, which is the MOST likely reason for this rule?

A. An inmate may be concealing a weapon in the bed.
B. A bed may be arranged to give the appearance of being occupied even when the inmate is not there.
C. Waking inmates for the count is a good disciplinary measure because it shows them that they are under constant guard.
D. It is important for officers on duty at night to have something to do to keep them busy.

9. *When counting a group of inmates on a work assignment, great care should be taken to insure accuracy. The count method should be adapted to the number of inmates and to the type of location.* 9.____

Suppose that you are supervising 15 inmates working in a kitchen. Most of them are moving about constantly, carrying dishes and equipment from one place to another. In order to make an accurate count, which of the following methods would be MOST suitable under these circumstances?

A. Have the inmates *freeze* where they are whenever you call for a count, even though some of them may be carrying hot pans or heavy stacks of dishes.
B. Have the inmates stop their work and gather in one place whenever it is necessary to make a count.
C. Circulate among the inmates and make an approximate count while they are working.
D. Divide the group into sections according to type of work and assign one inmate in each group to give you the number for this section.

10. *Officers on duty at entrances must exercise the greatest care to prevent movement of unauthorized persons. At vehicle entrances, all vehicles must be inspected and a record kept of their arrival and departure.* 10.____

Assume that, as a correction officer, you have been assigned to duty at a vehicle entrance. Which of the following is probably the BEST method of preventing the movement of unauthorized persons in vehicles?

A. If passenger identifications are checked when vehicle enters, no check is necessary when the vehicle leaves.
B. Passenger identifications should be checked for all vehicles when vehicle enters and when it leaves.

C. Passenger identifications need not be checked when vehicle enters, but should always be checked when vehicle leaves.
D. Except for official vehicles, passenger identifications should be checked when vehicle enters and when it leaves.

11. In making a routine search of an inmate's cell, an officer finds various items. Although there is no immediate danger, he is not sure whether the inmate is permitted to have one of the items. 11.___
Of the following, the BEST action for the officer to take is to

A. confiscate the item immediately
B. give the inmate the benefit of the doubt, and let him keep the item
C. consult his rule book or his supervising officer to find out whether the inmate is permitted to have the item
D. leave the item in the inmate's cell, but plan to report him for an infraction of the rules

12. *It is almost certain that there will be occasional escape attempts or an occasional riot or disturbance that requires immediate emergency action. A well-developed emergency plan for dealing with these events includes not only planning for prevention and control and planning for action during the disturbance, but also planning steps that should be taken when the disturbance is over.* 12.___

When a disturbance is ended, which of the following steps should be taken FIRST?

A. Punishing the ringleaders.
B. Giving first aid to inmates or other persons who were injured.
C. Making an institutional count of all inmates.
D. Adopting further security rules to make sure such an incident does not occur again.

13. *It is often important to make notes about an occurrence that will require a written report or personal testimony.* 13.___

Assume that a correction officer has made the following notes for the warden of the institution about a certain occurrence: *10:45 A.M. March 16, 2007. Cellblock A. Robert Brown was attacked by another inmate and knocked to the floor. Brown's head hit the floor hard. He was knocked out. I reported a medical emergency. Dr. Thomas Nunez came and examined Brown. The doctor recommended that Brown be transferred to the infirmary for observation. Brown was taken to the infirmary at 11:15 A.M.*
Which of the following important items of information is MISSING or is INCOMPLETE in these notes? The

A. time that the incident occurred
B. place where the incident occurred
C. names of both inmates involved in the fight
D. name of the doctor who made the medical examination

14. A correction officer has made the following notes for the warden of his institution about an incident involving an infraction of the rules: *March 29, 2007. Cellblock B-4. Inmates involved were A. Whitman, T. Brach, M. Purlin, M. Verey. Whitman and Brach started the trouble around 7:30 P.M. I called for assistance. Officer Haley and Officer Blair responded. Officer Blair got cut, and blood started running down his face. The bleeding looked very bad. He was taken to the hospital and needed eight stitches.* Which of the following items of information is MISSING or is INCOMPLETE in these notes? 14.____

A. The time and date of the incident
B. The place of the incident
C. Which inmates took part in the incident
D. What the inmates did that broke the rules

15. Your supervising officer has instructed you to follow a new system for handling inmate requests. It seems to you that the new system is not going to work very well and that inmates may resent it. What should you do? 15.____

A. Continue handling requests the old way but do not let your supervising officer know you are doing this.
B. Continue using the old system until you have a chance to discuss the matter with your supervising officer.
C. Begin using the new system but plan to discuss the matter with your supervising officer if the system really does not work well.
D. Begin using the new system but make sure the inmates know that it is not your idea and you do not approve of it.

16. *Inmates who are prison-wise may know a good many tricks for putting something over. For instance, it is an officer's duty to stop fights among inmates. Therefore, inmates who want to distract the officer's attention from something that is going on in one place may arrange for a phony fight to take place some distance away.* 16.____

To avoid being taken in by a trick like this, a correction officer should

A. ignore any fights that break out among inmates
B. always make an inspection tour to see what is going on elsewhere before breaking up a fight
C. be alert for other suspicious activity when there is any disturbance
D. refuse to report inmates involved in a fight if the fight seems to have been phony

17. *Copies of the regulations are posted at various locations in the cellblock so that inmates can refer to them.* 17.____

Suppose that one of the regulations is changed and the correction officers receive revised copies to post in their cellblocks. Of the following, the MOST effective way of informing the inmates of the revision is to

A. let the inmates know that you are taking down the old copies and putting up new ones in their place
B. post the new copies next to the old ones so that inmates will be able to compare them and learn about the change for themselves

C. leave the old copies up until you have had a chance to explain the change to each inmate
D. post the new copies in place of the old ones and also explain the change orally to the inmates

18. *A fracture is a broken bone. In a simple fracture, the skin is not broken. In a compound fracture, a broken end of the bone pierces the skin. Whenever a fracture is feared, the first thing to do is to prevent motion of the broken part.* 18.___

Suppose that an inmate has just tripped on a stairway and twisted his ankle. He says it hurts badly, but you cannot tell what is wrong merely by looking at it.
Of the following, the BEST action to take is to

A. tell the inmate to stand up and see whether he can walk
B. move the ankle gently to see whether you can feel any broken ends of bones
C. tell the inmate to rest a few minutes and promise to return later to see whether his condition has improved
D. tell the inmate not to move his foot and put in a call for medical assistance

19. *It is part of institutional procedure that at specified times during each 24-hour period all inmates in the institution are counted simultaneously. Each inmate must be counted at a specific place at a specified time. All movement of inmates ceases from the time the count starts until it is finished and cleared as correct.* 19.___

Assume that, as a correction officer, you are making such a count when an inmate in your area suddenly remembers he has an important 9 A.M. clinic appointment. You check his clinic pass and find that this is true.
What should you do?

A. Let him go to the clinic even though he may be counted again there.
B. Take him off your count and tell him to be sure he is included in the count being made at the clinic.
C. Keep him in your count and tell him to inform the officer at the clinic that he has already been counted.
D. Ask him to wait a few minutes until the counting period is over and then let him go to the clinic.

20. *Except in the case of a serious illness or injury (when a doctor should see the inmate immediately), emergency sick calls should be kept to a minimum, and inmates should be encouraged to wait for regular sick-call hours.* 20.___

In which of the following cases is an emergency sick call MOST likely to be justified?
A(n)

A. inmate has had very severe stomach pains for several hours
B. inmate has cut his hand, and the bleeding has now stopped
C. inmate's glasses have been broken, and he is nearly blind without them
D. normally healthy inmate has lost his appetite and does not want to eat

21. *People who have lost their freedom are likely to go through periods of depression or to become extremely resentful or unpleasant. A correction officer can help inmates who are undergoing such periods of depression by respecting their feelings and treating them in a reasonable and tactful manner.* 21.____

Suppose that an inmate reacts violently to a single request made in a normal, routine manner by a correction officer. Of the following, which is likely to be the MOST effective way of handling the situation?

A. Point out to the inmate that it is his own fault that he is in jail, and he has nobody to blame for his troubles but himself.
B. Tell the inmate that he is acting childishly and that he had better straighten out.
C. Tell the inmate in a friendly way that you can see he is feeling down, but that he should comply with your request.
D. Let the inmate know that you are going to report his behavior unless he changes his attitude.

22. An inmate tells you, a correction officer, of his concern about the ability of his wife and children to pay for rent and food while he is in the institution. 22.____
Of the following, which is the BEST action to take?

A. Assure him that his wife and children are getting along fine, although you do not actually know this.
B. Put him in touch with the social worker or the correction employee who handles such problems.
C. Offer to lend him money yourself if his family is really in need.
D. Advise him to forget about his family and start concentrating on his own problems.

23. *It is particularly important to notice changes in the general pattern of an inmate's behavior. When an inmate who has been generally unpleasant and who has not spoken to an officer unless absolutely necessary becomes very friendly and cooperative, something has happened, and the officer should take steps to make sure what.* 23.____

Of the following possible explanations for this change in behavior, which one is the LEAST likely to be the real cause?

A. The inmate may be planning some kind of disturbance or escape attempt and is trying to fool the officer.
B. The inmate may be trying to get on the officer's good side for some reason of his own.
C. His friendliness and cooperation may indicate a developing mental illness.
D. He may be overcoming his initial hostile reactions to his imprisonment.

24. As a correction officer, you have an idea about a new way for handling a certain procedure. Your method would require a minor change in the regulations, but you are sure it would be a real improvement. 24.____
The BEST thing for you to do is to

A. discuss the idea with your supervising officer, explaining why it would work better than the present method
B. try your idea on your own cellblock, telling inmates that it is just an experiment and not official

C. attempt to get officers on other cellblocks to use your methods on a strictly unofficial basis
D. forget the whole thing since it might be too difficult to change the regulations

25. *Correction officers assigned to visiting areas have a dual supervisory function since their responsibilities include receiving persons other than inmates, as well as handling inmates. Here, of all places, it is important for an officer to realize that he is acting as a representative of his institution and that what he is doing is very much like public relations work.* 25.____

Assume that you are a correction officer assigned to duty in a visiting area.
Which of the following ways of carrying out this assignment is MOST likely to result in good public relations? You should

A. treat inmates and visitors sternly because this will let them know that the institution does not put up with any nonsense
B. be friendly to inmates but suspicious of visitors
C. be stern with inmates but polite and tactful with visitors
D. treat both inmates and visitors in a polite but tactful way

KEY (CORRECT ANSWERS)

1. A
2. C
3. A
4. B
5. D
6. D
7. A
8. B
9. B
10. B
11. C
12. B
13. C
14. D
15. C
16. C
17. D
18. D
19. D
20. A
21. C
22. B
23. C
24. A
25. D

TEST 2

DIRECTIONS: Each question or incomplete statement is followed by several suggested answers or completions. Select the one that BEST answers the question or completes the statement. *PRINT THE LETTER OF THE CORRECT ANSWER IN THE SPACE AT THE RIGHT.*

Questions 1-5.

DIRECTIONS: Answer Questions 1 through 5 on the basis of the following passage.

The handling of supplies is an important part of correctional administration. A good deal of planning and organization is involved in purchase, stock control, and issue of bulk supplies to the cell-block. This planning is meaningless, however, if the final link in the chain – the cell-blook officer who is in charge of distributing supplies to the inmates – does not do his job in the proper way. First, when supplies are received, the officer himself should immediately check them or should personally supervise the checking, to make sure the count is correct. Nothing but trouble will result if an officer signs for 200 towels and discovers hours later that he is 20 towels short. Did the 20 towels "disappear," or did they never arrive in the first place? Second, all supplies should be locked up until they are actually distributed. Third, the officer must keep accurate records when supplies are issued. Complaints will be kept to a minimum if the officer makes sure that each inmate has received the supplies to which he is entitled, and if the officer can tell from his records when it is time to reorder to prevent a shortage. Fourth, the officer should either issue the supplies himself or else personally supervise the issuing. It is unfair and unwise to put an inmate in charge of supplies without giving him adequate supervision. A small thing like a bar of soap does not mean much to most people, but it means a great deal to the inmate who cannot even shave or wash up unless he receives the soap that is supposed to be issued to him.

1. Which one of the following jobs is NOT mentioned by the passage as the responsibility of a cellblock officer? 1.____

   A. Purchasing supplies
   B. Issuing supplies
   C. Counting supplies when they are delivered to the cellblock
   D. Keeping accurate records when supplies are issued

2. The passage says that supplies should be counted when they are delivered. Of the following, which is the BEST way of handling this job? 2.____

   A. The cellblock officer can wait until he has some free time and then count them himself.
   B. An inmate can start counting them right away, even if the cellblock officer cannot supervise his work.
   C. The cellblock officer can personally supervise an inmate who counts the supplies when they are delivered.
   D. Two inmates can count them when they are delivered, supervising each other's work.

3. The passage gives an example concerning a delivery of 200 towels that turned out to be 20 towels short. 3.___
The example is used to show that

   A. the missing towels were stolen
   B. the missing towels never arrived in the first place
   C. it is impossible to tell what happened to the missing towels because no count was made when they were delivered
   D. it does not matter that the missing towels were not accounted for because it is never possible to keep track of supplies accurately

4. The MAIN reason given by the passage for making a record when supplies are issued is that keeping records 4.___

   A. will discourage inmates from stealing supplies
   B. is a way of making sure that each inmate receives the supplies to which he is entitled
   C. will show the officer's superiors that he is doing his job in the proper way
   D. will enable the inmates to help themselves to any supplies they need

5. The passage says that it is unfair to put an inmate in charge of supplies without giving him adequate supervision. 5.___
Which of the following is the MOST likely explanation of why it would be *unfair* to do this?

   A. A privilege should not be given to one inmate unless it is given to all the other inmates too.
   B. It is wrong to make on inmate work when all the others can sit in their cells and do nothing.
   C. The cellblock officer should not be able to get out of doing a job by making an inmate do it for him.
   D. The inmate in charge of supplies could be put under pressure by other inmates to do them *special favors*.

Questions 6-10.

DIRECTIONS: Answer Questions 6 through 10 on the basis of the following passage.

The typical correction official must make predictions about the probable future behavior of his charges in order to make judgments affecting those individuals. In learning to predict behavior, the results of scientific studies of inmate behavior can be of some use. Most studies that have been made show that older men tend to obey rules and regulations better than younger men, and tend to be more reliable in carrying out assigned jobs. Men who had good employment records on the outside also tend to be more reliable than men whose records show haphazard employment or unemployment. Oddly enough, men convicted of crimes of violence are less likely to be troublemakers than men convicted of burglary or other crimes involving stealth. While it might be expected that first offenders would be much less likely to be troublemakers than men with previous convictions, the difference between the two groups is not very great. It must be emphasized, however, that predictions based on a man's background are only likelihoods – they are never certainties. A successful correction officer learns to give some weight to a man's background, but he should rely even more heavily on his own personal judgment of the individual in question. A good officer will develop in time a kind of sixth sense about human beings that is more reliable than any statistical predictions.

6. The passage suggests that knowledge of scientific studies of inmate behavior would PROBABLY help the correction officer to 6.____

   A. make judgments that affect the inmates in his charge
   B. write reports on all major infractions of the rules
   C. accurately analyze how an inmate's behavior is determined by his background
   D. change the personalities of the individuals in his charge

7. According to the information in the passage, which one of the following groups of inmates would tend to be MOST reliable in carrying out assigned jobs? 7.____

   A. Older men with haphazard employment records
   B. Older men with regular employment records
   C. Younger men with haphazard employment records
   D. Younger men with regular employment records

8. According to the information in the passage, which of the following are MOST likely to be troublemakers? 8.____

   A. Older men convicted of crimes of violence
   B. Younger men convicted of crimes of violence
   C. Younger men convicted of crimes involving stealth
   D. First offenders convicted of crimes of violence

9. The passage indicates that information about a man's background is 9.____

   A. a sure way of predicting his future behavior
   B. of no use at all in predicting his future behavior
   C. more useful in predicting behavior than a correction officer's expert judgment
   D. less reliable in predicting behavior than a correction officer's expert judgment

10. The passage names two groups of inmates whose behavior might be expected to be quite different, but who in fact behave only slightly differently. 10.____
    These two groups are

   A. older men and younger men
   B. first offenders and men with previous convictions
   C. men with good employment records and men with records of haphazard employment or unemployment
   D. men who obey the rules and men who do not

Questions 11-17.

DIRECTIONS: Questions 11 through 17 are based on the following pictures of objects found in Cells A, B, C, and D in a correctional institution.

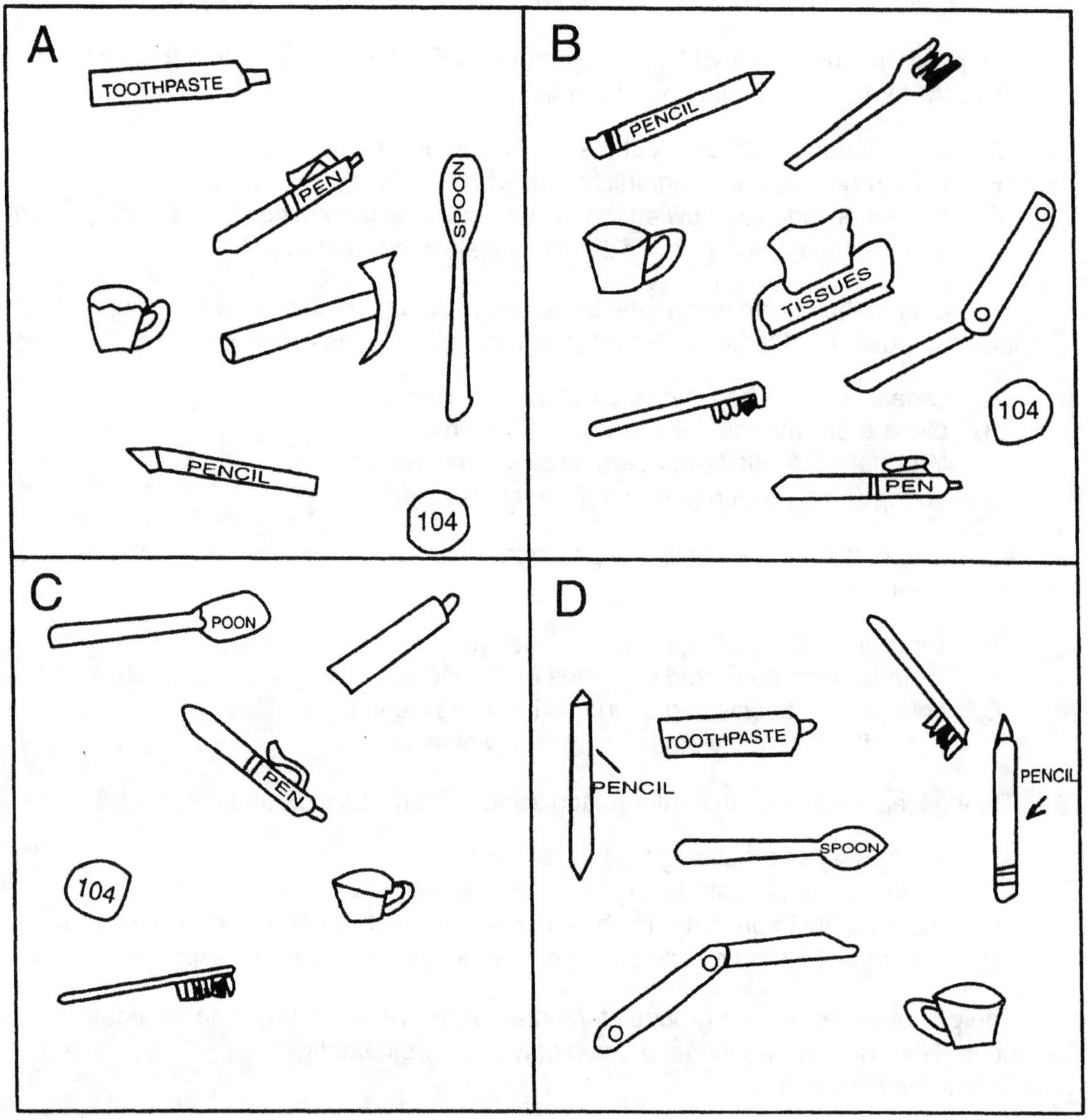

11. Which item can be found in every cell? 11.___

A. Cup B. Money C. Pencil D. Toothpaste

12. Which cell has toothpaste but no toothbrush? 12.___

A. A B. B C. C D. D

13. If knives and forks are prohibited in cells, how many cells are in violation of this rule? 13.___

A. 1 B. 2 C. 3 D. 4

14. One inmate failed to return his tool in the woodworking shop before returning to his cell. That inmate is in Cell 14.___

A. A B. B C. C D. D

15. The cell with the GREATEST number of objects is 15.____

A. A B. B C. C D. D

16. How many cells have AT LEAST one eating utensil? 16.____

A. 1 B. 2 C. 3 D. 4

17. Which cells contain money? 17.____

A. A, B, and C
B. A, B, and D
C. A, C, and D
D. B, C, and D

Questions 18-22.

DIRECTIONS: Answer Questions 18 through 22 on the basis of the following passage.

A large proportion of the people who are behind bars are not convicted criminals but people who have been arrested and are being held until their trial in court. Experts have often pointed out that this detention system does not operate fairly. For instance, a person who can afford to pay bail usually will not get looked up. The theory of the bail system is that the person will make sure to show up in court when he is supposed to since he knows that otherwise he will forfeit his bail -- he will lose the money he put up. Sometimes a person Who can show that he is a stable citizen with a job and a family will be released on "personal recognizance" (without bail). The result is that the well-to-do, the employed, and the family men can often avoid the detention system. The people who do wind up in detention tend to be the poor, the unemployed, the single, and the young.

18. According to the above passage, people who are put behind bars 18.____

A. are almost always dangerous criminals
B. include many innocent people who have been arrested by mistake
C. are often people who have been arrested but have not yet come to trial
D. are all poor people who tend to be young and single

19. The passage says that the detention system works *unfairly* against people who are 19.____

A. rich B. married C. old D. unemployed

20. The passage uses the expression *forfeit his bail*. Even if you have not seen the word *forfeit* before, you could figure out from the way it is used in the passage that *forfeiting* probably means ______ something. 20.____

A. losing track of
B. giving up
C. finding
D. avoiding

21. When someone is released on *personal recognizance*, this means that 21.____

A. the judge knows that he is innocent
B. he does not have to show up for a trial
C. he has a record of previous convictions
D. he does not have to pay bail

22. Suppose that two men were booked on the same charge at the same time, and that the same bail was set for both of them. One man was able to put up bail, and he was released. The second man was not able to put up bail, and he was held in detention. The reader of the passage would MOST likely feel that this result is 22.____

A. *unfair,* because it does not have any relation to guilt or innocence
B. *unfair,* because the first man deserves severe punishment
C. *fair,* because the first man is obviously innocent
D. *fair,* because the law should be tougher on poor people than on rich people

23. A certain cellblock has 240 inmates. From 8 A.M. to 9 A.M. on March 25, 120 inmates were assigned to cleanup work, and 25 inmates were sent for physical examinations. All the others remained in their cells. 23.____
How many inmates should have been in their cells during this hour?

A. 65 B. 85 C. 95 D. 105

24. There were 254 inmates in a certain cellblock at the beginning of the day. At 9:30 A.M., 12 inmates were checked out to the dispensary. At 10:00 A.M.,113 inmates were checked out to work details. At 10:30 A.M., 3 inmates were checked out to another cell-block. 24.____
How many inmates were present in this cellblock at 10:45 A.M. if none of the inmates who were checked out had returned?

A. 116 B. 126 C. 136 D. 226

25. There were 242 inmates in a certain cellblock at the beginning of the day. At 9:00 A.M., 116 inmates were checked out to a recreational program. At 9:15 A.M., 36 inmates were checked out to an educational program. At 9:30, 78 inmates were checked out on a work detail. By 10:15, the only inmates who had returned were 115 inmates who had been checked back in from the recreational program. A count made at 10:15 should show that the number of inmates present in the cellblock is 25.____

A. 127 B. 128 C. 135 D. 137

KEY (CORRECT ANSWERS)

1. A
2. C
3. C
4. B
5. D
6. A
7. B
8. C
9. D
10. B
11. A
12. A
13. B
14. A
15. B
16. D
17. A
18. C
19. D
20. B
21. D
22. A
23. C
24. B
25. A

READING COMPREHENSION
UNDERSTANDING AND INTERPRETING WRITTEN MATERIAL

EXAMINATION SECTION
TEST 1

DIRECTIONS: Each question or incomplete statement is followed by several suggested answers or completions. Select the one that BEST answers the question or completes the statement. *PRINT THE LETTER OF THE CORRECT ANSWER IN THE SPACE AT THE RIGHT.*

1. Custody in prison work used to be considered of such supreme importance that everything else was secondary. This statement implies MOST directly that 1.____

   A. formerly nothing was as important as custody in prison work
   B. formerly only custody was considered important in prison work
   C. today all aspects of prison work are considered equally important
   D. today reform of the prisoner is considered more important than custody

2. Since the total inmate treatment and training program is conditioned largely by custody requirements, its success is almost wholly dependent on flexibility of custody classification and handling of prisoners. 2.____
   Of the following, the MOST accurate statement based on the above statement is that the

   A. conditions of custody are completely dependent on the handling of inmates in accordance with their classification
   B. daily schedule at the institution should be flexible in order for the treatment and training program to succeed
   C. main factor influencing the inmate treatment and training program is the requirement for the proper safekeeping of inmates
   D. most important factor in the success of the treatment and training program is the cooperation of the inmates

3. An officer's revolver is a defensive and not offensive weapon. 3.____
   On the basis of this statement only, an officer should BEST draw his revolver to

   A. fire at an unarmed burglar
   B. force a suspect to confess
   C. frighten a juvenile delinquent
   D. protect his own life

4. Prevention of crime is of greater value to the community than the punishment of crime. 4.____
   If this statement is accepted as true, GREATEST emphasis should be placed on

   A. malingering
   B. medication
   C. imprisonment
   D. rehabilitation

5. The criminal is rarely or never reformed. Acceptance of this statement as true would mean that GREATEST emphasis should be placed on 5.____

   A. imprisonment
   B. parole
   C. probation
   D. malingering

6. Physical punishment of prison inmates has been shown by experience not only to be ineffective but to be dangerous and, in the long run, destructive of good discipline. According to the preceding statement, it is MOST reasonable to assume that, in the supervision of prison inmates, 6.____

A. a good correction officer would not use physical punishment
B. it is permissible for a good correction officer to use a limited amount of physical punishment to enforce discipline
C. physical punishment improves discipline temporarily
D. the danger of public scandal is basic in cases where physical punishment is used

7. There is no clear evidence that criminals, as a group, differ from non-criminals in their basic psychological needs. On the basis of this statement, it is MOST reasonable to assume that criminals and non-criminals 7.____

A. are alike in some important respects
B. are alike in their respective backgrounds
C. differ but slightly in all respects
D. differ in physical characteristics

8. Neither immediate protection for the community nor long-range reformation of the prisoner can be achieved by prison personnel who express toward the offender whatever feelings of frustration, fear, jealousy, or hunger for power they may have. Of the following, the CHIEF significance of this statement for correction officers is that, in their daily work, they should 8.____

A. be on the constant lookout for opportunities to prove their courage to inmates
B. not allow deeply personal problems to affect their relations with the inmates
C. not try to advance themselves on the job because of personal motives
D. spend a good part of their time examining their own feelings in order to understand better those of the inmates

9. Since ninety-five percent of prison inmates are released, and a great majority of these within two to three years, a prison which does nothing more than separate the criminal from society offers little promise of real protection to society. Of the following, the MOST valid reference which may be drawn from the preceding statement is that 9.____

A. once it has been definitely established that a person has criminal tendencies, that person should be separated for the rest of his life from ordinary society
B. prison sentences in general are much too short and should be lengthened to afford greater protection to society
C. punishment, rather than separation of the criminal from society, should be the major objective of a correctional prison
D. when a prison system produces no change in prisoners, and the period of imprisonment is short, the period during which society is protected is also short

10. A great handicap to successful correctional work lies in the negative response of the general community to the offender. Public attitudes of hostility toward, and rejection of, an ex-prisoner can undo the beneficial effects of even an ideal correctional system. Of the following, the CHIEF implication of this statement is that 10.____

A. a friendly community attitude will insure the successful reformation of the ex-prisoner
B. correctional efforts with most prisoners would generally prove successful if it were not for public hostility toward the former inmate
C. in the long run, even an ideal correctional system cannot successfully reform criminals
D. the attitude of the community toward an ex-prisoner is an important factor in determining whether or not an ex-prisoner reforms

11. While retribution and deterrence as a general philosophy in correction are widely condemned, no one raises any doubt as to the necessity for secure custody of some criminals.
Of the following, the MOST valid conclusion based on the preceding statement is that the 11.____

A. gradual change in the philosophy of correction has not affected custody practices
B. need for safe custody of some criminals is not questioned by anyone
C. philosophy of retribution, as shown in some correctional systems, has led to wide condemnation of custodial practices applied to all types of criminals

Questions 12-13.

DIRECTIONS: Questions 12 and 13 are to be answered SOLELY on the basis of the information contained in the following paragraph.

Those correction theorists who are in agreement with severe and rigid controls as a normal part of the correctional process are confronted with a contradiction; this is so because a responsibility which is consistent with freedom cannot be developed in a repressive atmosphere. They do not recognize this contradiction when they carry out their programs with dictatorial force and expect convicted criminals exposed to such programs to be reformed into free and responsible citizens.

12. According to the above paragraph, those correction theorists are faced with a contradiction who 12.____

A. are in favor of the enforcement of strict controls in a prison
B. believe that to develop a sense of responsibility, freedom must not be restricted
C. take the position that the development of responsibility consistent with freedom is not possible in a repressive atmosphere
D. think that freedom and responsibility can be developed only in a democratic atmosphere

13. According to the above paragraph, a repressive atmosphere in a prison 13.____

A. does not conform to present day ideas of freedom of the individual
B. is admitted by correction theorists to be in conflict with the basic principles of the normal correctional process

C. is advocated as the best method of maintaining discipline when rehabilitation is of secondary importance
D. is not suitable for the development of a sense of responsibility consistent with freedom

14. To state the matter in simplest terms, just as surely as some people are inclined to commit crimes, so some people are prevented from committing crimes by the fear of the consequences to themselves. 14.____
Of the following, the MOST logical conclusion based on this statement is that

A. as many people are prevented from committing criminal acts as actually commit criminal acts
B. most men are not inclined to commit crimes
C. people who are inclined to violate the law are usually deterred from their purpose
D. there are people who have a tendency to commit crimes and people who are deterred from crime

15. Probation is a judicial instrument whereby a judge may withhold execution of a sentence upon a convicted person in order to give opportunity for rehabilitation in the community under the guidance of an officer of the court. According to the preceding statement, it is MOST reasonable to assume that 15.____

A. a person on probation must report to the court at least once a month
B. a person who has been convicted of crime is sometimes placed on probation by the judge
C. criminals who have been rehabilitated in the community are placed on probation by the court after they are sentenced
D. the chief purpose of probation is to make the sentence easier to serve

Questions 16-19.

DIRECTIONS: Questions 16 through 19 are to be answered SOLELY on the basis of the following passage.

Traditional correctional institutions do not change or redirect the behavior of many of their inmates. Few of these establishments are equipped with adequate resources to treat the social and psychological handicaps of their wards. Too often, far removed ideologically from the world to which its charges must return, the institution often compounds the problems its corrective mechanisms are intended to cure. Training school academic programs, for example, range from poor to totally inadequate and usually reinforce negative feelings toward future learning experiences. Vocational programs are frequently designed to benefit the institution without regard to the inmate, and the usual low-key common denominator *treatment* program scarcely begins to meet the needs of many offenders.

Most correctional institutions must mobilize their limited resources in time and talent for purposes other than the ever-present concern about runaways or escapes. No one could quarrel rationally with the need to safeguard the community and control the behavior of people who may be of danger to themselves or others. It is ridiculous and tragic, however, that an overstated security approach is still the rule for the bulk of our correctional population.

16. The passage states that inmates of traditional correctional institutions are LIKELY to 16.____

    A. develop belief in radical political ideologies
    B. experience conditions that produce no betterment
    C. give major attention to devising plans of escape
    D. desire vocational training unrelated to their individual potential

17. The passage indicates that traditional training school academic programs lead inmates to 17.____

    A. adjust to the institutional setting
    B. avoid later formal learning
    C. develop respect for the values of education
    D. request more practical, vocational training

18. The passage indicates that most traditional correctional institutions, because of their ideological distance from the realities of the outside world, are MOST likely to 18.____

    A. ignore the safety of the outside community
    B. favor a minority of the inmate population
    C. lack properly motivated staff
    D. increase the problems of inmates

19. The passage states that the strong custodial function in most correctional institutions is MOST likely to be 19.____

    A. accorded excessive emphasis
    B. aimed at incorrigible inmates only
    C. necessary to redirect inmate behavior
    D. resented by the outside community

Questions 20-22.

DIRECTIONS: Questions 20 through 22 are to be answered SOLELY on the basis of the following passage.

The most widely accepted argument in favor of the death penalty is that the threat of its infliction deters people from committing capital offenses. Of course, since human behavior can be influenced through fear, and since man tends to fear death, it is possible to use capital punishment as a deterrent. But the real question is whether individuals think of the death penalty BEFORE they act, and whether they are thereby deterred from committing crimes. If for the moment we assume that the death penalty does this to some extent, we must also grant that certain human traits limit its effectiveness as a deterrent. Man tends to be a creature of habit and emotion, and when he is handicapped by poverty, ignorance, and malnutrition, as criminals often are, he becomes notoriously shortsighted. Many violators of the law give little thought to the possibility of detection and apprehension, and often they do not even consider the penalty. Moreover, it appears that most people do not regulate their lives in terms of the pleasure and pain that may result from their acts.

Human nature is very complex. A criminal may fear punishment, but he may fear the anger and contempt of his companions or his family even more, and the fear of economic insecurity or exclusion from the group whose respect he cherishes may drive him to commit the most daring crimes. Besides, fear is not the only emotion that motivates man. Love, loyalty, ambition, greed, lust, anger, and resentment may steel him to face even death in the perpetration of crime, and impel him to devise the most ingenious methods to get what he wants and to avoid detection.

If the death penalty were surely, quickly, uniformly, publicly, and painfully inflicted, it undoubtedly would prevent many capital offenses that are being committed by those who do consider the punishment that they may receive for their crimes. But this is precisely the point. Certainly, the way in which the death penalty has been administered in the United States is not fitted to produce this result.

20. Of the following, the MOST appropriate title for the above passage is 20.____

   A. CAPITAL OFFENSES IN THE UNITED STATES
   B. THE DEATH PENALTY AS A DETERRENT
   C. HUMAN NATURE AND FEAR
   D. EMOTION AS A CAUSE OF CRIME

21. The above passage implies that the death penalty, as it has been administered in the United States, 21.____

   A. was too prompt and uniform to be effective
   B. deterred many criminals who considered the possible consequences of their actions
   C. prevented crimes primarily among habitual criminals
   D. failed to prevent the commission of many capital offenses

22. According to the above passage, many violators of the law are 22.____

   A. intensely concerned with the pleasure or pain that may result from their acts
   B. influenced primarily by economic factors
   C. not influenced by the opinions of their family or friends
   D. not seriously concerned with the possibility of apprehension

Questions 23-25.

DIRECTIONS: Questions 23 through 25 are to be answered SOLELY on the basis of the information contained in the following paragraph.

As a secondary aspect of this revolutionary change in outlook resulting from the introduction of group counseling into the adult correctional institution, there must evolve a new type of prison employee, the true correctional or treatment worker. The top management will have to reorient their attitudes toward subordinate employees, respecting and accepting them as equal participants in the work of the institution. Rank may no longer be the measure of value in the inmate treatment program. Instead, the employee will be valuable whatever his location in the prison hierarchy or administrative plan in terms of his capacity constructively to relate himself to inmates as one human being to another. In group counseling, all employees must consider it their primary task to provide a wholesome environment for personality growth for the inmates in work crews, cell blocks, clerical pools, or classrooms. The above does not mean that custodial care and precautions regarding the prevention of disorders or escapes are cast aside or discarded by prison workers. On the contrary, the staff will be more acutely aware of the costs to the inmates of such infractions of institutional rules. Gradually, it is hoped, these instances of uncontrolled responses to over-powering feelings by inmates will become much less frequent in the treatment institution, In general, men in group counseling provide considerably fewer disciplinary infractions when compared with a control group of those still on a waiting list to enter group counseling, and especially fewer than those who do not choose to participate. It is optimistically anticipated that some day men in prison may have the same attitudes toward the staff, the same security in expecting treatment as do patients in a good general hospital.

23. According to the above paragraph, under a program of group counseling in an adult correctional institution, that employee will be MOST valuable in the inmate treatment program who 23.____

    A. can establish a constructive relationship of one human being to another between himself and the inmate
    B. gets top management to accept him as an equal participant in the work of the institution
    C. is in contact with the inmate in work crews, cell blocks, clerical pools or classrooms
    D. provides the inmate with a proper home environment for wholesome personality growth

24. According to the above paragraph, an effect that the group counseling program is expected to have on the problem of custody and discipline in a prison is that the staff will 24.____

    A. be more acutely aware of the cost of maintaining strict prison discipline
    B. discard old and outmoded notions of custodial care and the prevention of disorders and escapes
    C. neglect this aspect of prison work unless proper safeguards are established
    D. realize more deeply the harmful effect on the inmate of breaches of discipline

25. According to the above paragraph, a result that is expected from the group counseling method of inmate treatment in an adult correctional institution is 25.____

    A. a greater desire on the part of potential delinquents to enter the correctional institution for the purpose of securing treatment
    B. a large reduction in the number of infractions of institutional rules by inmates
    C. a steady decrease in the crime rate
    D. the introduction of hospital methods of organization and operation into the correctional institution

KEY (CORRECT ANSWERS)

1. A
2. C
3. D
4. D
5. A
6. A
7. A
8. B
9. D
10. D
11. B
12. A
13. D
14. D
15. B
16. B
17. B
18. D
19. A
20. B
21. D
22. D
23. A
24. D
25. B

TEST 2

DIRECTIONS: Each question or incomplete statement is followed by several suggested answers or completions. Select the one that BEST answers the question or completes the statement. *PRINT THE LETTER OF THE CORRECT ANSWER IN THE SPACE AT THE RIGHT.*

Questions 1-7.

DIRECTIONS: Questions 1 through 7 are to be answered on the basis of the following paragraph.

FLAGGING RULES

When a track gang is going to work under flagging protection at a given location, the Desk Trainmaster of the division must be notified. Work on trainways must not be performed on operating tracks between 6:00 A.M. and 9:00 A.M., or between 4:00 P.M. and 7:00 P.M. A flagman must be selected from the list of flagmen qualified as such by the Assistant General Superintendent. No person acting as a flagman may be assigned any duties other than those of a flagman. For underground flagging signals, lighted lanterns must be used. Out of doors, flags at least 23" x 29" in dimensions must be used between sunrise and sunset. Moving a red light across the track is the prescribed stop signal under normal flagging conditions. Moving a white light up and down means proceed slowly. A red light must never be used to give a proceed signal. Moving a yellow light up and down is a signal to a motorman to proceed very slowly. On the track to be worked on, two yellow lights must be displayed at a point not less than 500 feet, nor more than 700 feet, in approach to the flagman's station. On any track where caution lights are displayed, one green light must be displayed a safe distance beyond the farthest point of work. Caution lights must be displayed on the right hand side of the track.

1. Before starting work on a track, the transit official who should be notified is the 1.____

   A. General Superintendent
   B. Assistant General Superintendent
   C. Desk Trainmaster
   D. Yardmaster

2. It is permissible to start work on an operating track at 2.____

   A. 8 A.M. B. 11 A.M. C. 8 P.M. D. 6 P.M.

3. A flagman for a track gang MUST be selected from 3.____

   A. men on light duty
   B. disabled men
   C. a list of qualified men
   D. senior trackmen

4. The flagman who is protecting a working gang of trackmen 4.____

   A. should lend a hand when needed in heavy lifting
   B. should clean up the track area while awaiting trains
   C. must not be assigned to other duties
   D. can collect scrap iron while awaiting trains

5. The prescribed *stop* signal is given by moving a 5.____

   A. red light up and down
   B. green light up and down
   C. red light across the tracks
   D. green light across the tracks

6. The normal *proceed slowly* signal is given by moving a 6.___

A. red light up and down
B. white light up and down
C. yellow light across the tracks
D. green light across the tracks

7. Of the following, an ACCEPTABLE distance between a work area and the yellow lights is _______ feet. 7.___

A. 300 B. 600 C. 800 D. 1,000

Questions 8-12.

DIRECTIONS: Questions 8 through 12 are to be answered on the basis of the following passage.

The handling of supplies is an important part of correctional administration. A good deal of planning and organization is involved in purchase, stock control, and issue of bulk supplies to the cell-block. This planning is meaningless, however, if the final link in the chain -- the cell-block officer who is in charge of distributing supplies to the inmates -- does not do his job in the proper way. First, when supplies are received, the officer himself should immediately check them or should personally supervise the checking, to make sure the count is correct. Nothing but trouble will result if an officer signs for 200 towels and discovers hours later that he is 20 towels short. Did the 20 towels *disappear,* or did they never arrive in the first place? Second, all supplies should be locked up until they are actually distributed. Third, the officer must keep accurate records when supplies are issued. Complaints will be kept to a minimum if the officer makes sure that each inmate has received the supplies to which he is entitled, and if the officer can tell from his records when it is time to reorder to prevent a shortage. Fourth, the officer should either issue the supplies himself or else personally supervise the issuing. It is unfair and unwise to put an inmate in charge of supplies without giving him adequate supervision. A small thing like a bar of soap does not mean much to most people, but it means a great deal to the inmate who cannot even shave or wash up unless he receives the soap that is supposed to be issued to him.

8. Which one of the following jobs is NOT mentioned by the above passage as the responsibility of a cellblock officer? 8.___

A. Purchasing supplies
B. Issuing supplies
C. Counting supplies when they are delivered to the cell-block
D. Keeping accurate records when supplies are issued

9. The above passage says that supplies should be counted when they are delivered. Of the following, which is the BEST way of handling this job? 9.___

A. The cellblock officer can wait until he has some free time, and then count them himself.
B. An inmate can start counting them right away, even if the cellblock officer cannot supervise his work.
C. The cellblock officer can personally supervise an inmate who counts the supplies when they are delivered.
D. Two inmates can count them when they are delivered, supervising each other's work.

10. The above passage gives an example concerning a delivery of 200 towels that turned out to be 20 towels short. The example is used to show that 10.____

A. the missing towels were stolen
B. the missing towels never arrived in the first place
C. it is impossible to tell what happened to the missing towels because no count was made when they were delivered
D. it does not matter that the missing towels were not accounted for because it is never possible to keep track of supplies accurately

11. The MAIN reason given by the above passage for making a record when supplies are issued is that keeping records 11.____

A. will discourage inmates from stealing supplies
B. is a way of making sure that each inmate receives the supplies to which he is entitled
C. will show the officer's superiors that he is doing his job in the proper way
D. will enable the inmates to help themselves to any supplies they need

12. The above passage says that it is unfair to put an inmate in charge of supplies without giving him adequate supervision. 12.____
Which of the following is the MOST likely explanation of why it would be *unfair* to do this?

A. A privilege should not be given to one inmate unless it is given to all the other inmates too.
B. It is wrong to make one inmate work when all the others can sit in their cells and do nothing.
C. The cellblock officer should not be able to get out of doing a job by making an inmate do it for him.
D. The inmate in charge of supplies could be put under pressure by other inmates to do them *special favors*.

Questions 13-17.

DIRECTIONS: Questions 13 through 17 are to be answered on the basis of the following passage.

The typical correction official must make predictions about the probable future behavior of his charges in order to make judgments affecting those individuals. In learning to predict behavior, the results of scientific studies of inmate behavior can be of some use. Most studies that have been made show that older men tend to obey rules and regulations better than younger men, and tend to be more reliable in carrying out assigned jobs. Men who had good employment records on the outside also tend to be more reliable than men whose records show haphazard employment or unemployment. Oddly enough, men convicted of crimes of violence are less likely to be troublemakers than men convicted of burglary or other crimes involving stealth. While it might be expected that first offenders would be much less likely to be troublemakers than men with previous convictions, the difference between the two groups is not very great. It must be emphasized, however, that predictions based on a man's background are only likelihoods -- they are never certainties. A successful correction officer learns to give some weight to a man's background, but he should rely even more heavily on his own personal judgment of the individual in question. A good officer will develop in time a kind of sixth sense about human beings that is more reliable than any statistical predictions.

13. The above passage suggests that knowledge of scientific studies of inmate behavior would PROBABLY help the correction officer to 13.___

    A. make judgments that affect the inmates in his charge
    B. write reports on all major infractions of the rules
    C. accurately analyze how an inmate's behavior is determined by his background
    D. change the personalities of the individuals in his charge

14. According to the information in the above passage, which one of the following groups of inmates would tend to be MOST reliable in carrying out assigned jobs? 14.___

    A. Older men with haphazard employment records
    B. Older men with regular employment records
    C. Younger men with haphazard employment records
    D. Younger men with regular employment records

15. According to the information in the above passage, which of the following are MOST likely to be troublemakers? 15.___

    A. Older men convicted of crimes of violence
    B. Younger men convicted of crimes of violence
    C. Younger men convicted of crimes involving stealth
    D. First offenders convicted of crimes of violence

16. The above passage indicates that information about a man's background is 16.___

    A. a sure way of predicting his future behavior
    B. of no use at all in predicting his future behavior
    C. more useful in predicting behavior than a correction officer's expert judgment
    D. less reliable in predicting behavior than a correction officer's expert judgment

17. The above passage names two groups of inmates whose behavior might be expected to be quite different, but who in fact behave only slightly differently. 17.___
    These two groups are

    A. older men and younger men
    B. first offenders and men with previous convictions
    C. men with good employment records and men with records of haphazard employment or unemployment
    D. men who obey the rules and men who do not

Questions 18-22.

DIRECTIONS: Questions 18 through 22 are to be answered on the basis of the following passage.

A large proportion of the people who are behind bars are not convicted criminals, but people who have been arrested and are being held until their trial in court. Experts have often pointed out that this detention system does not operate fairly. For instance, a person who can afford to pay bail usually will not get locked up. The theory of the bail system is that the person will make sure to show up in court when he is supposed to since he knows that otherwise he will forfeit his bail -- he will lose the money he put up. Sometimes a person who can show that he is a stable citizen with a job and a family will be released on *personal recognizance* (without bail). The result is that the well-to-do, the employed, and the family men can often avoid the detention system. The people who do wind up in detention tend to be the poor, the unemployed, the single, and the young.

18. According to the above passage, people who are put behind bars 18.____

    A. are almost always dangerous criminals
    B. include many innocent people who have been arrested by mistake
    C. are often people who have been arrested but have not yet come to trial
    D. are all poor people who tend to be young and single

19. The above passage says that the detention system works UNFAIRLY against people 19.____

    A. rich B. married C. old D. unemployed

20. The above passage uses the expression *forfeit his bail.* Even if you have not seen the word *forfeit* before, you could figure out from the way it is used in the passage that *forfeiting* PROBABLY means _________ something. 20.____

    A. losing track of
    B. giving up
    C. finding
    D. avoiding

21. When someone is released on *personal recognizance,* this means that 21.____

    A. the judge knows that he is innocent
    B. he does not have to show up for a trial
    C. he has a record of previous convictions
    D. he does not have to pay bail

22. Suppose that two men were booked on the same charge at the same time, and that the same bail was set for both of them. One man was able to put up bail, and he was released. The second man was not able to put up bail, and he was held in detention. The reader of the above passage would MOST likely feel that this result is 22.____

    A. *unfair,* because it does not have any relation to guilt or innocence
    B. *unfair,* because the first man deserves severe punishment
    C. *fair,* because the first man is obviously innocent
    D. *fair,* because the law should be tougher on poor people than on rich people

Questions 23-25.

DIRECTIONS: Questions 23 through 25 are to be answered on the basis of the information contained in the following paragraph,

Group counseling may contain potentialities of an extraordinary character for the philosophy and especially the management and operation of the adult correctional institution. Primarily, the change may be based upon the valued and respected participation of the rank-and-file of employees in the treatment program. Group counseling provides new treatment functions for correctional workers. The older, more conventional duties and activities of correctional officers, teachers, maintenance foremen, and other employees, which they currently perform, may be fortified and improved by their participation in group counseling. Psychologists, psychiatrists, and classification officers may also need to revise their attitudes toward others on the staff and toward their own procedure in treating inmates to accord with the new type of treatment program which may evolve if group counseling were to become accepted practice in the prison. The primary locale of the psychological treatment program may move from the clinical center to all places in the institution where inmates are in contact with employees. The thoughtful guidance and steering of the program, figuratively its pilot-house, may still be the clinical center. The actual points of contact of the treatment program will, however, be wherever inmates are in personal relationship, no matter how superficial, with employees of the prison.

23. According to the above paragraph, a basic change that may be brought about by the introduction of a group counseling program into an adult correctional institution would be that the 23.____

   A. educational standards for correctional employees would be raised
   B. management of the institution would have to be selected primarily on the basis of ability to understand and apply the counseling program
   C. older and conventional duties of correctional employees would assume less importance
   D. rank-and-file employees would play an important part in the treatment program for inmates

24. According to the above paragraph, the one of the following that is NOT mentioned specifically as a change that may be required by or result from the introduction of group counseling in an adult correctional institution is a change in the 24.____

   A. attitude of the institution's classification officers toward their own procedures in treating inmates
   B. attitudes of the institution's psychologists toward correction officers
   C. place where the treatment program is planned and from which it is directed
   D. principal place where the psychological treatment program makes actual contact with the inmate

25. According to the above paragraph, under a program of group counseling in an adult correctional institution, treatment of inmates takes place 25.____

   A. as soon as they are admitted to the prison
   B. chiefly in the clinical center
   C. mainly where inmates are in continuing close and personal relationship with the technical staff
   D. wherever inmates come in contact with prison employees

KEY (CORRECT ANSWERS)

1. C
2. B
3. C
4. C
5. C
6. B
7. B
8. A
9. C
10. C
11. B
12. D
13. A
14. B
15. C
16. D
17. B
18. C
19. D
20. B
21. D
22. A
23. D
24. C
25. D

VOCABULARY
EXAMINATION SECTION
TEST 1

DIRECTIONS: In each of the following questions, select the lettered word or phrase which means MOST NEARLY the same as the word in capital letters. *PRINT THE LETTER OF THE CORRECT ANSWER IN THE SPACE AT THE RIGHT.*

1. INTERROGATE 1.____
   A. question B. arrest C. search D. rebuff

2. PERVERSE 2.____
   A. manageable B. poetic
   C. contrary D. patient

3. ADVOCATE 3.____
   A. champion B. employ C. select D. advise

4. APPARENT 4.____
   A. desirable B. clear C. partial D. possible

5. INSINUATE 5.____
   A. survey B. strengthen
   C. suggest D. insist

6. MOMENTOUS 6.____
   A. important B. immediate C. delayed D. short

7. AUXILIARY 7.____
   A. exciting B. assisting C. upsetting D. available

8. ADMONISH 8.____
   A. praise B. increase C. warn D. polish

9. ANTICIPATE 9.____
   A. agree B. expect C. conceal D. approve

10. APPREHEND 10.____
    A. confuse B. sentence C. release D. seize

11. CLEMENCY 11.____
    A. silence B. freedom C. mercy D. severity

12. THWART 12.____
    A. enrage B. strike C. choke D. block

13. RELINQUISH 13.____
    A. stretch B. give up C. weaken D. flee from

14. CURTAIL 14.____

A. stop B. reduce C. repair D. insult

15. INACCESSIBLE 15.____

A. obstinate B. unreachable
C. unreasonable D. puzzling

16. PERTINENT 16.____

A. related B. saucy C. durable D. impatient

17. INTIMIDATE 17.____

A. encourage B. hunt C. beat D. frighten

18. INTEGRITY 18.____

A. honesty B. wisdom
C. understanding D. persistence

19. UTILIZE 19.____

A. use B. manufacture
C. help D. include

20. SUPPLEMENT 20.____

A. regulate B. demand C. add D. answer

21. INDISPENSABLE 21.____

A. essential B. neglected
C. truthful D. unnecessary

22. ATTAIN 22.____

A. introduce B. spoil C. achieve D. study

23. PRECEDE 23.____

A. break away B. go ahead
C. begin D. come before

24. HAZARD 24.____

A. penalty B. adventure
C. handicap D. danger

25. DETRIMENTAL 25.____

A. uncertain B. harmful C. fierce D. horrible

KEY (CORRECT ANSWERS)

1. A
2. C
3. A
4. B
5. C
6. A
7. B
8. C
9. B
10. D
11. C
12. D
13. B
14. B
15. B
16. A
17. D
18. A
19. A
20. C
21. A
22. C
23. D
24. D
25. B

TEST 2

DIRECTIONS: In each of the following questions, select the lettered word or phrase which means MOST NEARLY the same as the word in capital letters. *PRINT THE LETTER OF THE CORRECT ANSWER IN THE SPACE AT THE RIGHT.*

1. AVARICE 1.____
   A. flight B. greed C. pride D. thrift

2. PREDATORY 2.____
   A. offensive B. plundering
   C. previous D. timeless

3. VINDICATE 3.____
   A. clear B. conquer C. correct D. illustrate

4. INVETERATE 4.____
   A. backward B. erect C. habitual D. lucky

5. DISCERN 5.____
   A. describe B. fabricate C. recognize D. seek

6. COMPLACENT 6.____
   A. indulgent B. listless C. overjoyed D. satisfied

7. ILLICIT 7.____
   A. insecure B. unclear C. unlawful D. unlimited

8. PROCRASTINATE 8.____
   A. declare B. multiply C. postpone D. steal

9. IMPASSIVE 9.____
   A. calm B. frustrated
   C. thoughtful D. unhappy

10. AMICABLE 10.____
    A. cheerful B. flexible C. friendly D. poised

11. FEASIBLE 11.____
    A. breakable B. easy
    C. likeable D. practicable

12. INNOCUOUS 12.____
    A. armless B. insecure C. insincere D. unfavorable

13. OSTENSIBLE 13.____
    A. apparent B. hesitant C. reluctant D. showy

14. INDOMITABLE 14.____

A. excessive
B. unconquerable
C. unreasonable
D. unthinkable

15. CRAVEN 15.____

A. cowardly B. hidden C. miserly D. needed

16. ALLAY 16.____

A. discuss B. quiet C. refine D. remove

17. ALLUDE 17.____

A. denounce B. refer C. state D. support

18. NEGLIGENCE 18.____

A. carelessness
B. denial
C. objection
D. refusal

19. AMEND 19.____

A. correct B. destroy C. end D. list

20. RELEVANT 20.____

A. conclusive
B. careful
C. obvious
D. related

21. VERIFY 21.____

A. challenge B. change C. confirm D. reveal

22. INSIGNIFICANT 22.____

A. incorrect
B. limited
C. unimportant
D. undesirable

23. SCURRILOUS 23.____

A. hideous B. abusive C. dirty D. illegal

24. PERPETRATE 24.____

A. indefinite
B. harass
C. solicit
D. commit

25. AMORPHOUS 25.____

A. shapeless
B. loving
C. debt-ridden
D. indecent

KEY (CORRECT ANSWERS)

1. B
2. B
3. A
4. C
5. C
6. D
7. C
8. C
9. A
10. C
11. D
12. A
13. A
14. B
15. A
16. B
17. B
18. A
19. A
20. D
21. C
22. C
23. B
24. D
25. A

TEST 3

DIRECTIONS: In each of the following questions, select the lettered word or phrase which means MOST NEARLY the same as the word in capital letters. *PRINT THE LETTER OF THE CORRECT ANSWER IN THE SPACE AT THE RIGHT.*

1. IMPLY 1.____

A. agree to B. hint at C. laugh at
D. mimic E. reduce

2. APPRAISAL 2.____

A. allowance B. composition C. prohibition
D. quantity E. valuation

3. DISBURSE 3.____

A. approve B. expend C. prevent
D. relay E. restrict

4. POSTERITY 4.____

A. back payment B. current procedure
C. final effort D. future generations
E. rare specimen

5. PUNCTUAL 5.____

A. clear B. honest C. polite
D. prompt E. prudent

6. PRECARIOUS 6.____

A. abundant B. alarmed C. cautious
D. insecure E. placid

7. FOSTER 7.____

A. delegate B. demote C. encourage
D. plead E. surround

8. PINNACLE 8.____

A. center B. crisis C. outcome
D. peak E. personification

9. COMPONENT 9.____

A. flattery B. opposite C. part
D. revision E. trend

10. SOLICIT 10.____

A. ask B. prohibit C. promise
D. revoke E. surprise

11. LIAISON 11.____

A. asset B. coordination C. difference
D. policy E. procedure

12. ALLEGE 12.____

A. assert B. break C. irritate
D. reduce E. wait

13. INFILTRATION 13.____

A. consumption B. disposal C. enforcement
D. penetration E. seizure

14. SALVAGE 14.____

A. announce B. combine C. prolong
D. save E. try

15. MOTIVE 15.____

A. attack B. favor C. incentive
D. patience E. tribute

16. PROVOKE 16.____

A. adjust B. incite C. leave
D. obtain E. practice

17. SURGE 17.____

A. branch B. contract C. revenge
D. rush E. want

18. MAGNIFY 18.____

A. attract B. demand C. generate
D. increase E. puzzle

19. PREPONDERANCE 19.____

A. decision B. judgment C. outweighing
D. submission E. warning

20. ABATE 20.____

A. assist B. coerce C. diminish
D. indulge E. trade

KEY (CORRECT ANSWERS)

1.	B	11.	B
2.	E	12.	A
3.	B	13.	D
4.	D	14.	D
5.	D	15.	C
6.	D	16.	B
7.	C	17.	D
8.	D	18.	D
9.	C	19.	C
10.	A	20.	C

TEST 4

DIRECTIONS: In each of the following questions, select the lettered word or phrase which means MOST NEARLY the same as, or the opposite of, the word in capital letters. *PRINT THE LETTER OF THE CORRECT ANSWER IN THE SPACE AT THE RIGHT.*

1. VINDICTIVE 1.____

   A. centrifugal B. forgiving C. molten
   D. tedious E. vivacious

2. SCOPE 2.____

   A. compact B. detriment C. facsimile
   D. potable E. range

3. HINDER 3.____

   A. amplify B. aver C. method
   D. observe E. retard

4. IRATE 4.____

   A. adhere B. angry C. authentic
   D. peremptory E. vacillate

5. APATHY 5.____

   A. accessory B. availability C. fervor
   D. pacify E. stride

6. LUCRATIVE 6.____

   A. effective B. imperfect C. injurious
   D. timely E. worthless

7. DIVERSITY 7.____

   A. convection B. slip C. temerity
   D. uniformity E. viscosity

8. OVERT 8.____

   A. laugh B. lighter C. orifice
   D. quay E. sly

9. SPORADIC 9.____

   A. divide B. incumbrance C. livid
   D. occasional E. original

10. RESCIND 10.____

    A. annul B. deride C. extol D. indulge E. insist

11. AUGMENT 11.____

    A. alter B. decrease C. obey
    D. perceive E. supersede

12. AUTONOMOUS 12.____

A. careless B. conceptual C. constant
D. defamatory E. independent

13. TRANSCRIPT 13.____

A. copy B. report C. sentence
D. termination E. verdict

14. DISCORDANT 14.____

A. astride B. comprised C. effusive
D. harmonious E. slick

15. DISTEND 15.____

A. constrict B. direct C. redeem
D. silence E. submerge

16. EMANATE 16.____

A. bridge B. coherency C. conquer
D. degrade E. flow

17. EXULTANT 17.____

A. easily upset B. in bad taste
C. in high spirits D. subject to moods
E. very much over-priced

18. PREVARICATE 18.____

A. hesitate B. increase C. lie
D. procrastinate E. reject

19. COGNIZANT 19.____

A. obvious B. search C. stupid
D. suspicious E. unaware

20. CREDIBLE 20.____

A. daring B. helpful C. surreptitious
D. unbelievable E. uncontrollable

KEY (CORRECT ANSWERS)

1. B
2. E
3. E
4. B
5. C
6. E
7. D
8. E
9. D
10. A
11. B
12. E
13. A
14. D
15. A
16. E
17. C
18. C
19. E
20. D

REPORT WRITING

EXAMINATION SECTION

TEST 1

DIRECTIONS: Each question or incomplete statement is followed by several suggested answers or completions. Select the one that BEST answers the question or completes the statement. *PRINT THE LETTER OF THE CORRECT ANSWER IN THE SPACE AT THE RIGHT.*

Questions 1-5.

DIRECTIONS: Questions 1 through 5 are to be answered on the basis of the Report of Offense that appears below.'

REPORT OF OFFENSE	Report No. 26743 Date of Report 10-12
Inmate *Joseph Brown*	
Age *27*	Number *61274*
Sentence *90 days*	Assignment *KU-187*
Place of offense *R.P.W. 4-1*	Date of offense *10/11/*
Offense Assaulting inmate	
Details *During 9:00 P.M., cellblock cleanup, inmate John Jones asked for pail being used by*	
Brown. Brown refused. Correction officer requested that Brown comply. Brown then threw	
pail at Jones with intent to injure him and said he would "get" Jones. Jones not hurt.	
Force used by officer *None*	
Name of reporting officer *R. Rodriguez*	No. *C-2056*
Name of superior officer *P. Ferguson*	

1. The person who made out this report is 1.____
   A. Joseph Brown B. John Jones
   C. R. Rodriguez D. P. Ferguson

2. Disregarding the details, the specific offense reported was 2.____
   A. insulting a fellow inmate B. assaulting a fellow inmate
   C. injuring a fellow inmate D. disobeying a correct officer

3. The number of the inmate who committed the offense is 3.____
   A. 26743 B. 61274 C. KU-187 D. CJ-2056

4. The offense took place on 4.____
   A. October 11 B. June 12 C. December 10 D. November 13

5. The place where the offense occurred is identified in the report as 5.____
   A. Brown's cell B. Jones' cell C. KU-187 D. R.P.W., 4-1

Questions 6-10.

DIRECTIONS: Questions 6 through 10 are to be answered on the basis of the Report of Loss or Theft that appears below.

REPORT OF LOSS OR THEFT	Date: *12/4*	*Time: 9:15 A.M.*
Complaint made by: *Richard Aldridge*		☐ Owner
306 S. Walter St.		☒ Other – explain:
		Head of Acctg. Dept.
Type of Property: *Computer*		Value: $450.00
Description: Dell Inspiron laptop		
Location: *768 N. Margin Ave., Accounting Dept. 3rd Floor*		
Time: *Overnight 12/3 – 12/4*		
Circumstances: *Mr. Aldridge reports he arrived at work 8:45 A.M., found office door open*		
and machine missing. Nothing else reported missing. I investigated and found signs of		
forced entry; door lock was broken.		
	Signature of Reporting Officer: *B.L. Ramirez*	
Notify:		
☐ Q Building & Grounds Office, 768 N. Margin Ave.		
☐ Q Lost Property Office, 110 Brand Ave. 0		
☒ Security Office, 703 N. Wide Street		

6. The person who made this complaint is 6.____
   A. a secretary B. a security officer
   C. Richard Aldridge D. B.L. Ramirez

7. The report concerns a computer that has been 7.____
   A. lost B. damaged C. stolen D. sold

8. The person who took the computer PROBABLY entered the office through 8.____
   A. a door B. a window
   C. the roof D. the basement

9. When did the head of the Accounting Department FIRST notice that the computer was missing? 9.____
   A. December 4 at 9:15 A.M. B. December 4 at 8:45 A.M.
   C. The night of December 3 D. The night of December 4

10. The event described in the report took place at 10.____
    A. 306 South Walter Street B. 768 North Margin Avenue
    C. 110 Brand Avenue D. 703 North Wide Street

Questions 11-15.

DIRECTIONS: Questions 11 through 15 are to be answered on the basis of the following excerpt from a recorded Annual Report of the Police Department. This material should be read first and then referred to in answering these questions, which are to be answered SOLELY on the basis of the material herein contained.

LEGAL BUREAU

One of the more important functions of this bureau is to analyze and furnish the department with pertinent information concerning Federal and State statutes and local laws which affect the department, law enforcement or crime prevention. In addition, all measures introduced in the State Legislature and the City Council, which may affect this department, are carefully reviewed by members of the Legal Bureau and, where necessary, opinions and recommendations thereon are prepared.

Another important function of this office is the prosecution of cases in the Magistrate's Courts. This is accomplished by assignment of attorneys who are members of the Legal Bureau to appear in those cases which are deemed to raise issues of importance to the department or questions of law which require technical presentation to facilitate proper determination; and also in those cases where request is made for such appearance by a magistrate, some other official of the city, or a member of the force. Attorneys are regularly assigned to prosecute all cases in the Family Court.

Proposed legislation was prepared and sponsored for introduction in the State Legislature and, at this writing, one of these proposals has already been enacted into law and five others are presently on the Governor's desk awaiting executive action. The new law prohibits the sale or possession of a hypodermic syringe or needle by an unauthorized person. The bureau's proposals awaiting executive action pertain to: an amendment to the Code of Criminal Procedure prohibiting desk officers from taking bail in gambling cases or in cases mentioned in Section 552, Code of Criminal Procedure, including confidence men and swindlers as jostlers in the Penal Law; prohibiting the sale of switch-blade knives of any size to children under 16 and bills extending the licensing period of gunsmiths.

The Legal Bureau has regularly cooperated with the Corporation Counsel and the District attorneys in respect to matters affecting this department, and has continued to advise and represent the Police Athletic League, the Police Sports Association, the Police Relief Fund, and the Police Pension Fund.

The following is a statistical report of the activities of the bureau during the current year as compared with the previous year:

	Current Year	Previous Year
Memoranda of law prepared	68	83
Legal matters forwarded to Corporation Counsel	122	144
Letters requesting legal information	756	807
Letters requesting departmental records	139	111
Matters for publication	17	26
Court appearances of members of bureau	4,678	4,621
Conferences	94	103
Lectures at Police Academy	30	33
Reports on proposed legislation	194	255
Deciphering of codes	79	27
Expert testimony	31	16
Notices to court witnesses	55	81
Briefs prepared	22	18
Court papers prepared	258	—

11. One of the functions of the Legal Bureau is to 11.____
    A. review and make recommendations on proposed federal laws affecting law enforcement
    B. prepare opinions on all measures introduced in the state legislature and the City Council
    C. furnish the Police Department with pertinent information concerning all new federal and state laws
    D. analyze all laws affecting the work of the Police Department

12. The Legal Bureau sponsored a bill that would 12.____
    A. extend the licenses of gunsmiths
    B. prohibit the sale of switch-blade knives to children of any size
    C. place confidence men and swindlers in the same category as jostlers in the Penal Law
    D. prohibit desk officers from admitting gamblers, confidence men, and swindlers to bail

13. From the report, it is NOT reasonable to infer that 13.____
    A. fewer bills affecting the Police Department were introduced in the current year
    B. the preparation of court papers was a new activity assumed in the current year
    C. the Code of Criminal Procedure authorizes desk officers to accept bail in certain cases
    D. the penalty for jostling and swindling is the same

14. According to the statistical report, the activity showing the GREATEST percentage of decrease in the current year compared with the previous year was 14.____
    A. matters for publication
    B. reports on proposed legislation
    C. notices to court witnesses
    D. memoranda of law prepared

15. According to the report, the percentage of bills prepared and sponsored by the Legal Bureau, which were passed by the State Legislature and sent to the Governor for approval, was 15.____
   A. approximately 3.2%
   B. approximately 2.6%
   C. approximately .5%
   D. not capable of determination from the data given

KEY (CORRECT ANSWERS)

1.	C	6.	C	11.	D
2.	B	7.	C	12.	C
3.	B	8.	A	13.	D
4.	A	9.	B	14.	A
5.	D	10.	B	15.	D

TEST 2

DIRECTIONS: Each question or incomplete statement is followed by several suggested answers or completions. Select the one that BEST answers the question or completes the statement. *PRINT THE LETTER OF THE CORRECT ANSWER IN THE SPACE AT THE RIGHT.*

Questions 1-2.

DIRECTIONS: Questions 1 and 2 are to be answered on the basis of the Instructions, the Bridge and Tunnel Officer's Toll Report form, and the situation given below. The questions ask how the report form should be filled in based on the Instructions and the information given in the situation.

INSTRUCTIONS

Assume that a Bridge and Tunnel Officer on duty in a toll booth must make an entry on the following report form immediately after each incident in which a vehicle driver does not pay the correct toll.

BRIDGE AND TUNNEL OFFICER'S TOLL REPORT			
Officer______		Date______	
Time	Type of Vehicle	Toll Collected	Explanation of Entry
1.______	______	______	______
2.______	______	______	______
______	______	______	______

SITUATION

John McDonald is a Bridge and Tunnel Officer assigned to toll booth 4, between the hours of 11 P.M. and 1 A.M.. On this particular tour, two incidents occurred. At 11:43 P.M., a five-axle truck stopped at the toll booth and Officer McDonald collected a $2.50 toll from the driver. As the truck passed, he realized the toll should have been $3.30, and he quickly copied the vehicle's license plate number as M724HJ. At 12:35 A.M., a motorcycle went through toll lane 4 without paying the toll. The motorcycle did not have any license plate.

1. The entry which should be made on line1 in the second column is 1.____
   A. 11:43 P.M.
   B. 12:34 A.M.
   C. five-axle truck
   D. motorcycle

2. The above passage does NOT provide the information necessary to fill in which of the following items? 2.____
   A. Officer
   B. Date
   C. Line 1, Toll Collected
   D. Line 2, Time

FACT SITUATION

Peter Miller is a Correction Officer assigned to duty in Cell-block A. His superior officer is John Doakes. Miller was on duty at 1:30 P.M. on March 21 when he heard a scream for help from Cell 12. He hurried to Cell 12 and found inmate Richard Rogers stamping out a flaming book of matches. Inmate John Jones was screaming. It seems that Jones had accidentally set fire to the entire book of matches while lighting a cigarette, and he had burned his left hand. Smoking was permitted at this hour. Miller reported the incident by phone, and Jones was escorted to the dispensary where his hand was treated at 2:00 P.M. by Dr. Albert Lorillo. Dr. Lorillo determined that Jones could return to his cellblock, but that he should be released from work for four days. The doctor scheduled a re-examination for March 22. A routine investigation of the incident was made by James Lopez. Jones confirmed to this officer that the above statement of the situation was correct,

REPORT OF INMATE INJURY	
(1) Name of Inmate	(2) Assignment
(3) Number	(4) Location
(5) Nature of Injury	(6) Date
(7) Details (how, when, where injury was incurred)	
(8) Received medical attention: date ________________	time________________
(9) Treatment	
(10) Disposition (check one or more):	
_____ (10-1) Return to housing area __(10-2) Return to duty	
_____ (10-3) Work release _____ days ____(10-4) Re-examine in _____ days	
(11) Employee reporting injury________________________________	
(12) Employee's supervisor or superior officer________________________	
(13) Medical officer treating injury____________________________	
(14) Investigating officer__________________________________	
(15) Head of institution__________________________________	

3. Which of the following should be entered in Item 1? 3.____
   A. Peter Miller
   B. John Doakes
   C. Richard Rogers
   D. John Jones

4. Which of the following should be entered in Item 11? 4.____
   A. Peter Miller
   C. James Lopez
   C. Richard Rogers
   D. John Jones

5. Which of the following should be entered in Item 8? 5.____
   A. 2/21, 1:30 P.M.
   B. 2/21, 2:00 P.M.
   C. 3/21, 1:30 P.M.
   D. 3/21, 2:00 P.M.

6. For Item 10, which of the following should be checked? 6.____
   A. 10-4 only
   B. 10-1 and 10-4
   C. 10-1, 10-3, and 10-4
   D. 10-2, 10-4, and 10-4

7. Of the following items, which one CANNOT be filled in on the basis of the information given in the Fact Situation? Item 7.____
   A. 12 B. 13 C. 14 D. 15

Questions 8-11.

DIRECTIONS: Questions 8 through 11 are to be answered on the basis of the Fact Situation and the Traffic Control Report form below. Read the Fact Situation carefully, and examine the blank report form. The questions ask how the report form should be filled in based on the information given in the Fact Situation.

FACT SITUATION

Mary Fields is a Traffic Control Agent. Her City Employee Number is Z90019. She is assigned to duty at the intersection of Silver Street and Amber Avenue. On the morning of May 15, she arrives at this intersection at 9:00 A.M. and sees that there is a new *patch job* on the surface of Amber Avenue in the middle of the pedestrian crosswalk and near the northwest corner of the intersection. They day before, an emergency crew was digging here. The hole is now closed and resurfaced, but the patch job on the surface was not done very well. The patch is nearly an inch higher than the surrounding surface, and it has a sharp edge that pedestrians are likely to trip on. Mary Fields thinks this condition is dangerous, and she reports it on the Traffic Control Report form.

TRAFFIC CONTROL REPORT
DEFECTIVE EQUIPMENT OR UNSAFE CONDITION

1. Date of observation ______________________ 2. Time______________________
3. Exact location____
4. Type of equipment or condition found to be defective or unsafe______________
5. Type of defect____
6. Name of reporting Agent_______________________________________
7. Employee No.______________________ 8. Precinct No.________________

---

8. Which of the following should be entered in Blank 3? 8.____
   A. Silver Street at Amber Avenue, near northwest corner
   B. Silver Street at Amber Avenue, near northwest corner
   C. Amber Avenue at Silver Street, near northeast corner
   D. Amber Avenue at Silver Street, near northwest corner

9. Which of the following should be entered in Blank 4? 9.____
   A. Pedestrian traffic signals
   B. Pedestrian crosswalk markings
   C. Surface patch
   C. Unsafe condition

10. The information called for in Blank 5 is needed to determine what kind of repairs must be made and what kind of repair crew must be sent. 10.____
Which of the following entries for Blank 5 will be MOST useful to the people who receive this report in deciding what kind of repair crew to assign to the job?
   A. Pedestrians may stumble and fall.
   B. New patch is higher than rest of surface.
   C. Emergency crew dug a hole here.
   D. Street repairs were not done very well.

11. There is one blank on the form for which the Fact Situation does not provide the information needed. 11.____
The blank that CANNOT be filled out on the basis of the information given is Blank
   A. 2   B. 6   C. 7   D. 8

Questions 12-15.

DIRECTIONS: Questions 12 through 15 are to be answered on the basis of the Fact Situation and the Report of Arrest form below. Questions ask how the report form should be filled in based on the information given in the Fact Situation.

FACT SITUATION

Jesse Stein is a special officer (security officer) who is assigned to a welfare center at 435 East Smythe Street, Brooklyn. He was on duty there Thursday morning, February 1. At 10:30 A.M., a client named Jo Ann Jones, 40 years old, arrived with her 10-year-old son Peter. Another client, Mary Alice Wiell, 45 years old, immediately began to insult Mrs Jones. When Mrs. Jones told her to go away, Mrs. Wiell pulled out a long knife. The special officer (security officer) intervened and requested Mrs. Wiell to drop the knife. She would not, and he had to use necessary force to disarm her. He arrested her on charges of disorderly conduct, harassment, and possession of a dangerous weapon. Mrs. Wiell lives at 118 Heally Street, Brooklyn, Apartment 4F, and she is unemployed. The reason for her aggressive behavior is not known.

REPORT OF ARREST	
(01)	(08)
(Prisoner's surname)(first)(initial)	(Precinct)
(02)	(09)
(Address)	(Date of Arrest – Month, Day)
(03) (04) (05)	(10)
(Date of Birth) (Age) (Sex)____	(Time of arrest)
(06)______________(07)______________	(11)
(Occupation) (Where employed)	(Place of arrest)
(12)______________________________	
(Specific offenses)________________	
(13)______________________	(14)______________________
(Arresting officer)	(14) Officer's No.)

12. What entry should be made in Blank 01? 12.____
    A. Jo Ann Jones
    B. Jones, Jo Ann
    C. Mary Wiell
    D. Wiell, Mary A.

13. Which of the following should be entered in Blank 04? 13.____
    A. 40
    B. 40's
    C. 45
    D. Middle-aged

14. Which of the following should be entered in Blank 09? 14.____
    A. Wednesday, February 1, 10:30 A.M.
    B. February 1
    C. Thursday morning, February 2
    D. Morning, February 4

15. Of the following, which would be the BEST entry to make in Blank 11? 15.____
    A. Really Street Welfare Center
    B. Brooklyn
    C. 435 e. Smythe St., Brooklyn
    D. 118 Heally St., Apt. 4F

KEY (CORRECT ANSWERS)

1.	C	6.	C	11.	D
2.	B	7.	D	12.	D
3.	D	8.	D	13.	C
4.	A	9.	C	14.	B
5.	D	10.	B	15.	C

ARITHMETICAL REASONING EXAMINATION SECTION TEST 1

DIRECTIONS: Each question or incomplete statement is followed by several suggested answers or completions. Select the one that BEST answers the question or completes the statement. *PRINT THE LETTER OF THE CORRECT ANSWER IN THE SPACE AT THE RIGHT.*

1. Multiply $38.85 by 2; then subtract $27.90. The CORRECT answer is: 1.____

   A. $21.90 B. $48.70 C. $49.80 D. $50.70

2. Add $53.66, $9.27, and $18.75; then divide by 2. The CORRECT answer is: 2.____

   A. $35.84 B. $40.34 C. $40.84 D. $41.34

3. Out of 192 inmates in a certain cellblock, 96 are to go on a work detail and another 32 are to report to a vocational class. All the rest are to remain in the cellblock. How many inmates should be left on the cellblock? 3.____

   A. 48 B. 64 C. 86 D. 128

4. Assume that you are responsible for seeing that the right number of utensils are counted out for a meal. You need enough utensils for 620 men. One fork and one spoon are needed for each man. In addition, one ladle is needed for each group of 20 men. How many utensils will be needed altogether? 4.____

   A. 1,240 B. 1,271 C. 1,550 D. 1,860

5. Assume that you are supervising the inmates who are assigned to a dishwashing detail. There is an inverse relationship between the amount of time it takes to do all the dishwashing and the number of inmates who are washing dishes. When two inmates are washing dishes, the job takes six hours. If there are four inmates washing dishes, how long should the job take? ______ hour(s). 5.____

   A. 1 B. 2 C. 3 D. 4

6. A certain cellblock has 240 inmates. From 8 A.M. to 9 A.M. on March 25, 120 inmates were assigned to cleanup work and 25 inmates were sent for physical examinations. All the others remained in their cells. How many inmates should have been in their cells during this hour? 6.____

   A. 65 B. 85 C. 95 D. 105

7. There were 254 inmates in a certain cellblock at the beginning of the day. At 9:30 A.M., 12 inmates were checked out to the dispensary. At 10:00 A.M., 113 inmates were checked out to work details. At 10:30 A.M., 3 inmates were checked out to another cellblock. How many inmates were present in this cellblock at 10:45 A.M. if none of the inmates who were checked out had returned? 7.____

   A. 116 B. 126 C. 136 D. 226

8. There were 242 inmates in a certain cellblock at the beginning of the day. At 9:00 A.M., 116 inmates were checked out to a recreational program. At 9:15, 36 inmates were checked out to an educational program. At 9:30, 78 inmates were checked out on a work detail. By 10:15, the only inmates who had returned were 115 inmates who had been checked back in from the recreational program.
A count made at 10:15 should show that the number of inmates present in the cell-block is 8.___

A. 127 B. 128 C. 135 D. 137

9. If an officer's weekly salary is increased from $400 to $450, then the percent of increase is ______ percent. 9.___

A. 10 B. 11 1/9 C. 12 1/2 D. 20

10. Suppose that one-half the officers in a department have served for more than ten years and one-third have served for more than 15 years.
Then, the fraction of officers who have served between ten and fifteen years is 10.___

A. 1/3 B. 1/5 C. 1/6 D. 1/12

11. In a prison, there are four floors on which prisoners are housed. The top floor houses one-quarter of the inmates, the bottom floor houses one-sixth of the inmates, and one-third are houses on the second floor. The rest of the inmates are housed on the third floor.
If there are 90 inmates housed on the third floor, the TOTAL number of inmates housed on all four floors together is 11.___

A. 270 B. 360 C. 450 D. 540

12. Assume that you are in charge of supervising the laundry sorting and counting. You expect that on a certain day there will be nearly 7,000 items to be sorted and counted. If one inmate can sort and count 500 items in an hour, how many inmates are needed to sort all 7,000 items in one hour? 12.___

A. 2 B. 5 C. 7 D. 14

13. A carpentry course is being given for inmates who want to learn a skill. The course will be taught in several different groups. Each group should contain at least 12 but not more than 16 men. The smaller the group, the better, as long as there are at least 12 men per group.
If 66 inmates are going to take the course, they should be divided into ______ groups of ______. 13.___

A. 4; 16 men
B. 4; 13 men and 1 group of 14 men
C. 3; 13 men and 2 groups of 14 men
D. 6; 11 men

14. Of the 100 inmates in a certain cellblock, one-half were assigned to cleanup work, and one-fifth were assigned to work in the laundry.
How many inmates were NOT assigned for cleanup work or laundry work? 14.___

A. 30 B. 40 C. 50 D. 60

15. A certain cellblock has a maximum capacity of 250 inmates. On March 26, there were 200 inmates housed in the cellblock. 12 inmates were added on that day, and 17 inmates were added on the following day. No inmates left on either day. How many more inmates could this cellblock have accommodated on the second day? 15.____

A. 11 B. 16 C. 21 D. 28

16. Suppose that ten percent of those who commit serious crimes are convicted and that fifteen percent of those convicted are sentenced for more than 3 years. The percentage of those committing serious crimes who are sentenced for more than 3 years is ______ percent. 16.____

A. 15 B. 1.5 C. .15 D. .015

17. Assume that there are 1,100 employees in a city agency. Of these, 15 percent are officers, 80 percent of whom are attorneys; of the attorneys, two-fifths have been with the agency over five years. Then, the number of officers who are attorneys and have over five years experience with the agency is MOST NEARLY 17.____

A. 45 B. 53 C. 132 D. 165

18. An employee who has 500 cartons of supplies to pack can pack them at the rate of 50 an hour. After this employee has worked for half an hour, he is joined by another employee who can pack 45 cartons an hour. Assuming that both employees can maintain their respective rates of speed, then the TOTAL number of hours required to pack all the cartons is 18.____

A. 4 1/2 B. 5 C. 5 1/2 D. 6 1/2

19. Thirty-six officers can complete an assignment in 22 days. Assuming that all officers work at the same rate of speed, the number of officers that would be needed to complete this assignment in 12 days is 19.____

A. 42 B. 54 C. 66 D. 72

Questions 20-22.

DIRECTIONS: Questions 20 through 22 are to be answered on the basis of the table below. Data for certain categories have been omitted from the table. You are to calculate the missing numbers if needed to answer the questions.

	2007	2008	Numerical Increase
Correction Officers	1,226	1,347	
Court Attendants		529	34
Deputy Sheriffs	38	40	
Supervisors			
	2,180	2,414	

20. The number in the *Supervisors* group in 2007 was MOST NEARLY 20.____

A. 500 B. 475 C. 450 D. 425

21. The LARGEST percentage increase from 2007 to 2008 was in the group of 21.____

A. Correction Officers
B. Court Attendants
C. Deputy Sheriffs
D. Supervisors

22. In 2008, the ratio of the number of Correction Officers to the total of the other three categories of employees was MOST NEARLY 22.____

A. 1:1 B. 2:1 C. 3:1 D. 4:1

23. If an officer's weekly salary is increased from $640.00 to $720.00, then the percent of increase is ______ percent. 23.____

A. 10 B. 11 1/9 C. 12 1/2 D. 20

24. Suppose that one-half the officers in a department have served for more than ten years and one-third have served for more than 15 years. 24.____
If there are 150 officers In the department, how many have served less than 10 years?

A. 25 B. 50 C. 75 D. 100

25. Moving radar can allow a trooper to clock the speed of an oncoming vehicle. 25.____
If the radar shows a combined speed of 140 mph and the patrol car Is cruising at 65mph, how fast is the oncoming vehicle traveling? ______ mph.

A. 205 B. 85 C. 75 D. 65

KEY (CORRECT ANSWERS)

1. C
2. C
3. B
4. B
5. C
6. C
7. B
8. A
9. C
10. C
11. B
12. D
13. B
14. A
15. C
16. B
17. B
18. C
19. C
20. D
21. D
22. A
23. C
24. A
25. C

SOLUTIONS TO PROBLEMS

1. ($38.85)(2) = $77.70, and $77.70 - $27.90 = $49.80
2. $53.66 + $9.27 + $18.75 = $81.68, and $81.68 ÷ 2 = $40.84
3. 192 - 96 - 32 = 64 left in the cellblock
4. Number of forks and spoons combined = (620)(2) = 1240

   Number of ladles = 620 ÷ 20 = 31

   Total number of utensils = 1271
5. Time needed = (2/4)(6 hrs.) = 3 hrs. Note that the number of inmates varies inversely with the time needed.
6. 240 - 120 - 25 = 95 inmates in their cells
7. 254 - 12 - 113 - 3 = 126 present at 10:45 AM
8. 242 - 116 - 36 - 78 + 115 = 127 present at 10:15 AM
9. Percent increase $(\frac{\$50}{\$400})(100)=12\frac{1}{2}\%$
10. 1/2-1/3=1/6 have served between 10 and 15 years
11. 1-1/4-1/6-1/3=1/4 of all inmates are housed on the 3rd floor. Number of inmates on all floors = 90 ÷ 1/4 = 360
12. 7000 ÷ 500 = 14 inmates needed
13. The best grouping is 4 groups of 13 and 1 group of 14.
14. 1 - 1/2 - 1/5 = 3/10 and (3/10)(100) = 30
15. 250 - 200 - 12 - 17 = 21 more inmates
16. (.10)(.15) = .015 = 1.5% sentenced for more than 3 years
17. $(1100)(.15)(.80)(2/5) = 52.8 \approx 53$
18. During the 1st half-hour, 25 cartons have been packed. The number of additional hours needed = 475 ÷ (50+45) = 5. Total time = 5 1/2 hrs.
19. (36)(22) = 792 officer-days. Then, 792 ÷ 12 days = 66 officers
20. Number of court attendants in 2007 = 529 - 34 = 495

    Number of supervisors in 2007 = 2180 - 495 - 1226 - 38 = 421, closest to 425
21. % increase for correction officers, court attendants, deputy sheriffs, and supervisors = $=\frac{121}{1226}\text{x}100, \frac{34}{495}\text{x}100, \frac{2}{38}\text{x}100$, and $\frac{77}{421}\text{x}100$, respectively, which becomes (approx.) 9.9%,6.9%, 5.3%, and 18.3%. The group with the largest percent increase is supervisors. (Note: Number of supervisors in 1988 is 498)
22. 1347 : (2414-1347) = 1347 : 1067 ≈ 1.26:1, closest to 1:1
23. $\frac{\$80}{\$640}=\frac{1}{8}=12\frac{1}{2}\%$ increase
24. 1 - 1/2 = 1/2 have served fewer than 10 years. Then, (150)(1/2) = 75. 1/3 of 150 = 50 more than 15 yrs. 150 - (75+50) = 25 remaining (assuming each group is mutually exclusive)
25. 140 - 65 = 75 mph

TEST 2

DIRECTIONS: Each question or incomplete statement is followed by several suggested answers or completions. Select the one that BEST answers the question or completes the statement. *PRINT THE LETTER OF THE CORRECT ANSWER IN THE SPACE AT THE RIGHT.*

1. An investigator uses Forms A, B, and C in filling out his investigation reports. He uses Form B five times as often as Form A, and he uses Form C three times as often as Form If the total number of all forms used by the investigator in a month equals 735, how many times was Form B used? 1.____

   A. 150 B. 175 C. 205 D. 235

2. Of all the investigators in one agency, 25% work in a particular building. Of these, 12% have desks on the 14th floor. 2.____
   What percentage of the investigators work in this building but do NOT have desks on the 14th floor?

   A. 12% B. 13% C. 22% D. 23%

3. An investigator is given 2 reports to read. Report P is 160 pages long and takes the investigator 3 hours and 20 minutes to read. 3.____
   If Report S is 264 pages long and the investigator reads it at the same rate as he reads Report P, how long will it take him to read Report S?
   ______ hours ______ minutes.

   A. 4; 15 B. 4; 50 C. 5; 10 D. 5; 30

4. A team of 6 investigators was assigned to interview 234 people. 4.____
   If half the investigators conduct twice as many interviews as the other half, and the slow group interviews 12 persons a day, how many days would it take to complete this assignment?
   ______ days.

   A. 4 1/4 B. 5 C. 6 D. 6 1/2

5. The investigators in one agency conduct an average of 12 interviews an hour from 10 M. to 12 Noon and from 1 P.M. to 5 P.M. daily. The director of this agency knows from past experience that 20% of those called in to be interviewed are unable to keep the appointments that were scheduled. 5.____
   If the director wants his staff to be kept occupied with interviews for the entire time period that has been set aside for this function, how many appointments should be scheduled for each day?

   A. 86 B. 90 C. 96 D. 101

6. An investigator has a 430-page report to read. The first day he is able to read 20 pages. The second day he reads 10 pages more than the first day, and the third day he reads 15 pages more than the second day. 6.____
   If on the following days he continues to read at the same rate he was reading on the third day, he will COMPLETE the report on the ______ day.

   A. 7th B. 8th C. 10th D. 11th

7. The 36 investigators in an agency are each required to submit 25 investigation reports a week. These reports are filled out on a certain form, and only one copy of the form is needed per report. 7.____
Allowing 20% for wastage, how many packages of 45 forms a piece should be ordered for each weekly period?

A. 15 B. 20 C. 25 D. 30

8. During the month, an investigative unit received $260 for stationery and telephone expenditures. It spent 43% for stationery and 1/3 of the balance for telephone service. The amount of money that was left at the end of the month was MOST NEARLY 8.____

A. $49 B. $50 C. $99 D. $109

9. Suppose a badly cracked sidewalk, 160 feet long and 14 feet wide, is to be torn up and replaced in four equal sections. 9.____
Each section will measure ______ square feet.

A. 40 B. 220 C. 560 D. 680

10. A businessman pays R dollars a month in rent, has a weekly payroll of P dollars, and a utility bill of U dollars for each two months. 10.____
His annual expenses can be expressed by

A. 12(R+P+U)
B. 52(R+P+U)
C. 12 R+52P+6U
D. 12(R+4P+2U)

11. An interviewer can interview P number of people in H number of hours, including the time needed to prepare a report on each interview. 11.____
The number of people he can interview in a work week of W hours is represented by

A. HW/p B. PW/H C. PH/W D. 35H/p

12. Claims investigated by a certain unit total $8,430,000 for the year. 12.____
If the cost of investigating these claims is 17.3 cents per $100, the yearly cost of investigating these claims is MOST NEARLY

A. $1,450 B. $14,500 C. $145,000 D. $1,450,000

13. Suppose that a certain agency had a 2005 budget of $1,100,500. The 2006 budget was 7% higher than that of 2005, and the 2007 budget was 8% higher than that of 2006. 13.____
Of the following, which one is MOST NEARLY that agency's budget for 2007?

A. $1,117,624
B. $1,261,737
C. $1,265,575
D. $1,271,738

14. Suppose that on a scaled drawing of an office building floor, 1/2 inch represents three feet of actual floor dimensions. 14.____
A floor which is, in fact, 75 feet wide and 132 feet long has which of the following dimensions on this scaled drawing?
______ inches wide and ______ inches long.

A. 9.5; 20.5
B. 12.5; 22
C. 17; 32
D. 25; 44

15. In 2009, the number of investigations completed in a certain unit had increased 230 over the number completed in 2008, an increase of 10%. In 2010, the number completed decreased 10% from the number completed in 2009. Therefore, the number of investigations completed in 2010 was ______ the number completed in 2008. 15.____

A. 23 less than
B. 123 less than
C. 230 more than
D. the same as

16. Assume that during a certain period Unit A investigated 400 cases and Unit B investigated 300 cases. 16.____
If each unit doubled its number of investigations, the proportion of Unit A's investigations to Unit B's investigations would then be ______ it was.

A. twice what
B. one-half as large as
C. one-third larger than
D. the same as

17. In a certain family, the teenage daughter's annual earnings are 5/8 the earnings of her brother and 1/5 the earnings of her father. 17.____
If her brother earns $19,200 a year, then her father's annual earnings are

A. $60,000 B. $75,000 C. $80,000 D. $96,000

18. Assume that, of the 1,700 verifications made by a certain investigating unit in a one week period, 40% were birth records, 30% were military records, 10% were citizenship records, and the remainder were miscellaneous records. Then the MOST accurate of the following statements about the relative number of different records is that 18.____

A. citizenship records verifications equaled 20% of military record verifications
B. fewer than 700 verifications were birth records
C. miscellaneous records verifications were 20% more than citizenship records verifications
D. more than 550 verifications were military records

19. Two units, A and B, answer respectively 1,000 and 1,500 inquiries a month. 19.____
Assuming that the number of inquiries answered by Unit A increase at the rate of 20 each month, while those answered by Unit B decrease at the rate of 5 each month, the two units will answer the same number of inquiries at the end of ______ months.

A. 10 B. 15 C. 20 D. 25

20. Assume that the XYZ Company has $10,402.72 cash on hand. If it pays $699.83 of this for rent, the amount of cash on hand would be 20.____

A. $9,792.89 B. $9,702.89 C. $9,692.89 D. $9,602.89

21. On January 31, Mr. Warren's checking account had a balance of $933.68. 21.____
If he deposited $36.40 on February 2, $126.00 on February 9, and $90.02 on February 16 and wrote no checks during this period, what was the balance of his account on February 17?

A. $680.26 B. $681.26 C. $1,186.10 D. $1,187.00

22. If the city department of purchase bought 190 calculators for $79.35 each and 208 calculators for $83.99 each, the TOTAL price paid for these calculators is 22.____

A. $31,581.30 B. $32,546.42
C. $33,427.82 D. $33,586.30

23. Subtract: 95,432 23.____
67,596

A. 27,836 B. 27,846 C. 27,936 D. 27,946

24. Add: 1/2 + 5/7 = 24.____

A. 1 3/14 B. 1 2/7 C. 1 5/14 D. 1 3/7

25. Suppose that an employee's monthly pension benefit is computed by dividing 3/5 of his final year's salary by 12. If an employee retires after earning $19,000 in his final year, his monthly pension benefit will be 25.____

A. $840 B. $850 C. $890 D. $950

KEY (CORRECT ANSWERS)

1. B
2. C
3. D
4. D
5. B

6. D
7. C
8. C
9. C
10. C

11. B
12. B
13. D
14. B
15. A

16. D
17. A
18. B
19. C
20. B

21. C
22. B
23. A
24. A
25. D

SOLUTIONS TO PROBLEMS

1. Let x = number of times using Form B; 1/5x = number of times using Form A; 3x = number of times using Form C. Then, 1/5x + x + 3x = 735. Solving, x = 175
2. (.25)(1-.12) = 22% work in this building but do not have desks on the 14th floor.
3. 160 pgs/200 min. = .8 page per minute. Then, 264/.8 = 330 min. = 5 hrs. 30 min.
4. 3 investigators interview 12 people per day while the other 3 investigators interview 24 people per day. Finally, 234 ÷ (12+24) = 6 1/2 days
5. Number of appointments = (12)(2+4)/.80 = 90
6. Let x = number of days in which he can read at the same rate as that on the 3rd day. We have: 1st day = 20 pgs., 2nd day = 30 pgs., 3rd day = 45 pgs. Then, 20 + 30_+ 45x = 430. Solving, x = $8.\overline{4}$. Finally, he will need $8.\overline{4} + 2 = 10.\overline{4}$ days to complete the reading, i.e., the 11th day.
7. (36)(25) = 900 forms with no waste. Allowing for a 20% waste factor, 900 ÷ .80 = 1125 forms will be needed. Number of packages needed = 1125 ÷ 45 = 25
8. 43% was spent for stationery, and (1/3)(57%) = 19% was spent for telephone service. Amount left = (1-.43-.19)($260) = $98.80 ≈ $99
9. (160 ft.)(14 ft.)/4 = 560 sq.ft.
10. Annual expenses = 12R + 52P + 6U
11. Let x = number of people interviewed in W hrs. Then, $\frac{P}{H} = \frac{X}{W}$ Solving, x = PW/H
12. $8,430,000 ÷ $100 = 84,300. Then, (84,300)(.173) = $14,583.90, which is closest to $14,500 in the selections.
13. Budget for 2007 = ($1,100,500)(1.07)(1.08) ≈ $1,271,738
14. (75/3)(1/2") = 12.5" wide, and (132/3)(1/2") = 22" long
15. Number of investigations in 2008 = 230 ÷ 10% = 2300
Number of investigations in 2009 = 2300 + 230 = 2530
Number of investigations in 2010 = (2530X.90) = 2277
Finally, 2277 represents 23 less than 2300.
16. New numbers would be 800 and 600 for Units A and B, respectively. Then, 800/600 = 4:3 = 400/300. The new ratio equals the old ratio.
17. Daughter's earnings = (5/8) ($19,200) = $12,000. Then, the father's earnings = $12,000 ÷ 1/5 = $60,000
18. (.40)(1700) = 680 birth records, which is less than 700.
19. Let x = number of months. Then, 1000 + 20x = 1500 - 5x Solving, x = 20
20. $10,402.72 - $699.83 = $9702.89
21. $933.68 + $36.40 + $126.00 + $90.02 = $1186.10
22. (190)($79.35) + (208)($83 .99) = $32,546.42
23. 95,432 - 67,596 = 27,836
24. 1/2 + 5/7 = 7/14 + 10/14 = 17/14 = 1 3/14
25. Monthly pension benefit = (3/5) ($19,000) ÷ 12 = $950

TEST 3

DIRECTIONS: Each question or incomplete statement is followed by several suggested answers or completions. Select the one that BEST answers the question or completes the statement. *PRINT THE LETTER OF THE CORRECT ANSWER IN THE SPACE AT THE RIGHT.*

1. A certain store is selling cloth table napkins. The small size costs 35¢ each or 99¢ for a package of 3. The large size costs 55¢ each or $1.59 for a package of 3. 1.____
   The LOWEST possible price for 11 large napkins and 10 small ones is

   A. $4.03 B. $8.99 C. $9.19 D. $11.13

2. Children's sweaters were sold in a certain store for $13.95 each. They were then placed on sale at 40% off. 2.____
   If a woman bought 3 sweaters on sale and was charged $24.11 (excluding sales tax), she was

   A. charged the correct price
   B. overcharged $7.37
   C. undercharged $1.00
   D. undercharged $17.74

3. Assume you check the weight of all the packages of meat in a certain supermarket. Of the 585 packages tested, 40% are shortweight. Of the shortweight packages, 15% are shortweight by 10% or more. 3.____
   The number of packages of meat that are shortweight by 10% or more is MOST NEARLY

   A. 22 B. 23 C. 35 D. 52

4. A certain car rental agency charges $27.00 a day and 30¢ a mile, but gives a 15% discount to anyone renting a car for 1 week or more. 4.____
   If one man rents a car for 3 days and drives 375 miles, and another man rents a car for 9 days and drives 775 miles, the total cost for the two rentals will be MOST NEARLY

   A. $234.84 B. $597.00 C. $605.10 D. $669.00

5. Of the 435 boxes of Brand X cookies on the shelves in a certain supermarket, 31% are more than 5% shortweight. Of the remaining boxes, 18% weigh over 5% more than they should. 5.____
   The number of boxes that fall within 5% of the correct weight is MOST NEARLY

   A. 164 B. 213 C. 222 D. 246

6. Convert 4/9 to a decimal. Carry your work to four decimal places. 6.____

   A. .4445 B. .4455 C. .4444 D. .4454

7. Convert 1/2% to a fraction. 7.____

   A. 1/2 B. 1/200 C. 1/50 D. 1/5

8. What percent is $75 of $575. Carry your work to four decimal places. 8.____

   A. 1304 B. 13.0434 C. 13 D. 130.4

9. An invoice amounts to $1,875 less 10% and 10%; terms 2/10 net 30. It is paid within the discount period. 9.____
What is the NET amount of the check?

A. $1,488.38 B. $1,488.37 C. $1,500 D. $1,470

10. The Bon Bon Company buys candy at $1.60 a pound. 10.____
At what price per pound should candy be marked in order to sell at a discount of 20% from the marked price and still make a profit of 20% on the selling price?

A. $2.50 B. $2.60 C. $2.70 D. $2.80

11. A washing machine and a dishwashing machine were sold for $240 each. The clothes washer was sold at a loss of 25% of cost, and the dishwasher at a gain of 25% of cost. 11.____
How much was gained or lost on the entire transaction,or did the dealer break even?

A. $32 loss
B. $20 gain
C. $48 gain
D. No gain or loss

12. Three pipes fill a pool of water. One pipe can fill it alone in 6 hours, another in 8 hours, and a third in 12 hours. 12.____
How many hours will be used to fill the pool if all pipes are opened at the same time?

A. 8 2/3 B. 2 2/3 C. 26 D. 7 1/3

13. If 10 men working 8 hours a day can do a job in 3 days, how many days are needed if 6 men work 10 hours a day? 13.____

A. 4 B. 5 C. 3 1/2 D. 5 1/2

14. The Dunn Company gave each employee a bonus to be determined as follows: 15% on that part of his salary which is $30,000 or less, 10% on that part of his salary greater than $30,000 and up to and including $60,000,5% on that part of his salary over $60,000. Mr. Smith, an employee, received a bonus of $8,250. Find his basic salary. 14.____

A. $37,500 B. $47,500 C. $62,500 D. $75,000

15. A freight train leaves New York for Buffalo at 9:00 P.M. and travels at the rate of 30 miles an hour. At 12:00 Midnight of the same day, on the same railroad, a passenger train leaves New York for Buffalo and travels at 54 miles an hour. 15.____
The passenger train will overtake the freight train at APPROXIMATELY ______ A.M.

A. 6:45 B. 3:22 C. 3:45 D. 4:54

16. A salesman gets a commission of 6% on his sales. 16.____
If he wants his commission to amount to $720, he will have to sell merchandise totaling

A. $1,420 B. $12,000 C. $1,200 D. $120

17. A merchant purchased a suit for $240.00 and sold it for $320.00. 17.____
The mark-up on the cost price is

A. 25% B. 33 1/3% C. 75% D. 15%

18. Assume that out of a shipment of 135 crates of oranges, 11 crates of oranges do not meet acceptable standards. The percentage of crates of oranges which meet acceptable standards is MOST NEARLY 18.____

A. 8.1% B. 12.3% C. 87.7% D. 91.9%

19. Assume that a shipment of 35 cases of goods, each containing 72 packages, is to be returned to the manufacturer if more than 3% of the packages prove to be defective. The maximum number of defective packages the shipment may contain in order for it NOT to be rejected is 19.____

A. 74
B. 75
C. 76
D. none of the above

20. Assume that two shipments of goods arrive at a warehouse. The first shipment contains 280 boxes, each measuring 4" x 8" x 10". The second shipment contains 94 cartons, each measuring 1' x 1' x 4'. 20.____
The total number of cubic feet required to store both shipments is MOST NEARLY

A. 428 B. 466 C. 804 D. 992

21. Assume that an agency uses 700 reams of bond paper per month and that it must have a three-month supply of bond paper on hand at all times. It takes 2 1/2 months from the time a supply of bond paper is ordered to the time it is delivered. 21.____
What is the MINIMUM re-order point?

A. 800 B. 1,750 C. 3,100 D. 3,850

22. A dietician wishes to order enough butter to serve 2,300 school children at lunch time. 15% of the children will take two pats of butter; 10% of the children will take no butter; the remainder will take one pat of butter. Each pat of butter weighs 3/16 of an ounce. APPROXIMATELY how many pounds of butter should the dietician order? (Allow no butter for wastage.) 22.____

A. 16 B. 29 C. 35 D. 41

23. By taking advantage of a series discount of 4%, 3%, and 2%, respectively, a buyer paid $7.17 less than list price for an article. 23.____
The list price of the article was MOST NEARLY

A. $78 B. $79 C. $81 D. $82

24. 572 divided by .52 is 24.____

A. 1100 B. 110 C. 11.10 D. 11.00

25. The number of decimal places in the product of 0.4266 and 0.3333 is 25.____

A. 8 B. 6 C. 4 D. 2

KEY (CORRECT ANSWERS)

1. C
2. C
3. C
4. B
5. D
6. C
7. B
8. B
9. C
10. A
11. A
12. B
13. A
14. D
15. C
16. B
17. B
18. D
19. B
20. A
21. D
22. B
23. D
24. A
25. A

SOLUTIONS TO PROBLEMS

1. 11 large napkins cost (3)($1.59) + (2)(.55) = $5.87
   10 small napkins cost (3)(.99) + (1)(.35) = $3.32
   Total minimum cost = $9.19
2. On sale, the cost of 3 sweaters = (3)($13.95)(.60) = $25.11 Therefore, this woman was undercharged $1.00
3. (585)(.40)(.15) = 35.1 ≈ 35
4. Cost for 1st man = (3)($27.00) + (375)(.30) = $193.50
   Cost for 2nd man = [(9)($27.00)+(775)(.30)](.85) = $404.18 Total cost = $597.68, which is closest to $597.00 among the selections.
5. (435)(.31) ≈ 135 more than 5% shortweight. Also, of the remaining 300 boxes, (.18)(300) = 54 are more than 5% overweight. Thus, 435 - 135 - 54 = 246 fall within 5% of the correct weight.
6. $4/9 = .\overline{4} = .4444$
7. 1/2% = 1/2•1/100 = 1/200
8. $\frac{\$75}{\$575} = \frac{3}{23} \approx 13.04\%$
9. ($1875)(.90)(.90) = $1518.75, which is closest to $1500 among the selections
10. Let x = marked price. Then, x - .20x = selling price. So, x - .20x - $1.60 = .20(x-.20x). Simplifying this equation, .80x - 1.60 = .20x - .04x. Solving, x = $2.50
11. Total selling price = (2)(240) = $480. Cost of clothes washer = $240 ÷ .75 = $320, and the cost of dishwasher = $240 ÷ 1.25 = $192. Total cost of these 2 items = $512, so that the loss = $512 - $480 = $32
12. Let x = number of hours. Then, (1/6)(x) + (1/8)(x) + (1/12x) = 1 Simplifying, 3/8x = 1. Solving, x = 2 2/3
13. (10)(8)(3) = 240 man-hours. Then, 240 ÷ 6 ÷ 10 = 4 days
14. If his salary were $30,000, his bonus = ($30,000)(.15) = $4500. If his salary were $60,000, his bonus = $4500 + (.10)($60,000-$30,000) = $7500. Thus, his salary exceeds $60,000. His bonus of $8250 exceeds $7500 by $750. If x = his basic salary, then (.05)(x-$60,000) = $750. Solving, x = $75,000
15. Let x = number of hours of travel for the passenger train. Then, 30(x+3) = 54x. Solving, x = 3.75 = 3 hrs. 45 min. The actual time is 3:45 AM.
16. $720 ÷ .06 = $12,000 worth of merchandise
17. $80/$240 = 33 1/3%
18. 124/135 ≈ 91.9%
19. (35)(72)(.03) = 75.6. So, 75 would be the highest allowable number of defectives.
20. (280)(4/12)(8/12)(10/12) + (94)(1)(1)(4) ≈ 428 cu.ft.
21. (700)(3+2 1/2) = 3850 reams
22. Number of pats needed = (2300)(.15)(2) + (2300)(.75)(1) = 2415. Number of ounces = (2415)(3/16) ≈ 453. Finally, number of pounds = 453 ÷ 16 ≈ 28
23. Let x = list price. Then, x - (x)(.96)(.97)(.98) = $7.17 Solving, x ≈ $82

24. $572 \div .52 = 1100$
25. $(.4266)(.3333)$ = an answer with 8 decimal places.
    Actual answer = .14218578

POLICE SCIENCE NOTES
DETENTION PROCEDURES

Introduction

Generally detention is thought of as confinement of a prisoner in a jail facility from his formal booking to his formal release. This includes a period of time when he is merely held for bail or court appearance, when he is held after trial for formal sentencing, and when he is actually serving time in a jail or prison. Actually his arrest restricts or removes his freedom and places him under official restraint; thus, it is at this point that his actual detention begins.

Responsibility for the prisoner before booking may be solely that of the arresting officer or it may be given over to jail personnel assigned to transport him to the detention facility. We are concerned, therefore, as a practical matter with the entire time the prisoner is in official custody beginning with his arrest and ending with his release from custody.

Security is the essence of detention and implies assurance against escape or rescue of the prisoner. It also implies a full measure of personal safety for the officers, the prisoner himself, other inmates and visitors and other citizens.

Although it has been implied, and is true in fact, that our concern is with persons arrested for the commission of crimes, our responsibility is a broader one. The more broad responsibility will be increasingly important in time of natural disaster or civil defense emergency. The latter includes the "holding" for safekeeping of the mentally and physically incompetent, children without parents or who are lost or abandoned, persons who are threatened by mobs or individuals, and those who must be held as material witnesses. While legal and procedural provisions must be made to handle each of the above, this is a local matter not detailed here.

Transportation

Usually an arresting officer makes a search of his prisoner at the time of arrest for dangerous weapons,means of self-destruction, and less frequently, for evidence of a crime. Officers should be trained and required to make this search. Nonetheless, since it is often made under unusual conditions of stress, transporting and booking officers should also conduct searches with final responsibility lying with the booking officer. Adequate search is a protection to police and jailers, to the prisoner and other inmates, and to visitors and other citizens.

The search, however, only removes one kind of danger; the security measure of adequate restraint must be provided to avoid loss of the prisoner by his own actions or those of others. The restraint is also provided, of course, as another means of preventing injury to the prisoner and to others.

Transportation should be considered as any means used to get the prisoner from one point to another which is usually considered to be from the location of arrest to the place of detention. Transportation, however, is also involved in taking the prisoner to court, in moving him from one place of detention to another, and in taking him to the site of work details or assignments. For our purposes we must assume that transportation may mean moving the prisoner on foot, in a special or regular police automobile, in a special prisoner vehicle (paddywagon or prisoner van) or by other means including aircraft or boats.

The same general precautions apply to all means of transport because the need for security and restraint exists in all. Transport by walking should only be considered in the absence of a proper vehicle, for very short distances, or when physical circumstances may require it, as in moving the prisoner from a detention facility to a court. The number of officers required varies according to apparent need but also according to prescribed regulations. Only one officer is required in the transport of noncriminal nonviolent persons in protective custody and these include children, the aged, minor offenders, and others. Two officers should be used normally for a person under criminal arrest if there is even a nominal possibility of escape or rescue. Three or more officers should be used in serious criminal cases, cases involving a violent prisoner, or where there is likely to be a serious attempt to escape, rescue, or attack the prisoner.

Two officers should almost always be used in prisoner transport by vehicle except in minor cases when the prisoner is placed in a separate, secure and specially designed section of the vehicle screened off from the driver. When a vehicle is used all doors should be locked and inside handles removed from the prisoner section, as in the rear of an automobile.

Minimal restraint is required when the prisoner is in a secure and separate section of the vehicle unless conflict among prisoners may develop. Reasonable restraint should be used otherwise and will usually involve the use of handcuffs. Whenever handcuffs and other restraining devices are required public display of their use should be avoided.

Special precautions should be used at the place of detention because this is the most likely point of escape or rescue. It is important that detention officers assist transporting officers in placing prisoners in the detention facility. Although the prisoner has been under restraint since his arrest, detention in a formal sense begins when he is placed in the detention facility. Properly booking and admitting the prisoner is of utmost importance and carefully prescribed admittance procedures should be established and followed. The latter, of course, must conform to State and local legal requirements. A prisoner's property, and evidence also, must be properly identified, receipted, and secured. Identification of property should be witnessed under most circumstances and especially when the prisoner is unable to sign for it. Securing property implies controlling it so that it may be returned intact on the prisoner's release.

Fingerprinting and photographing of each prisoner should be required in all criminal cases and in emergency conditions where accurate identification is important as when the prisoner is suffering from amnesia. Exceptions to this practice may be established, i.e., if the prisoner had been previously arrested and his identification established prior to the present arrest.

A final detailed and complete search must be made. The search should be for evidence if this is appropriate under the circumstances; however, the principal purpose at this point is probably to remove offensive weapons and means of self-destruction. Before a prisoner is placed in a cell it should be carefully searched also.

Capabilities for medical examination of incoming prisoners, especially those who are sick or injured, should be provided. This is not only humane but may prevent serious problems later including criticism for failure to provide proper care. Under some circumstances a detailed medical examination for all prisoners may be practicable. In this case, by formal regulation, prisoners falling in certain categories must be examined. Categories should include any person over 60 years of age as this age group will usually contain a much higher percentage of persons requiring care than would those who are younger; any person with a history of illness or disability known to the officers by prior acquaintance with the person or through medical records he carries on his person; any person who is apparently, although not necessarily obviously, ill or injured; any prisoner who complains of illness or injury; and any person who is unconscious or comatose.

It is standard practice in detention facilities to provide for separation of prisoners by age and sex. Quite obviously juveniles and adults should not be quartered together, nor should men be placed with women. Those who have communicable diseases or who may have been exposed to them should be placed in quarantine sections. Those who are perverts or who exhibit tendencies to perversion should be separated from others, particularly children. Those who are mentally deranged, or who apparently become so, must also be isolated. This may be an especially important consideration under emer-gency conditions. Less serious offenders should be separated from the more serious offenders to avoid recruiting prisoners to the ranks of major criminals. The use of psychiatrists and medical personnel is recommended to assist in determining necessary separation in the case of perversion and mental derangement.

Providing adequate security is essential. All offensive weapons and means of self-destruction must be physically protected and adequately guarded. None should be within reach of any prisoner. Guards should not carry firearms while in any prisoner section. Full control of all means of entrance and exit must be provided. No guard should have on his person a set of keys which would allow escape from or admittance to the full facility or a series of its sections. All tools require close control because they may be used as weapons, escape devices, or provide the means to make such items. Prisoners being returned to cells from corridors, shops, and dining rooms should be searched.

Medical supplies must be carefully controlled. Their possession by prisoners provide means of self-destruction and barter. Under some circumstances prisoners would maliciously destroy essential medical provisions.

On a frequent, intermittent basis, quarters and inmates must be inspected and prisoners counted.

To avoid emotional problems, provide exercise, and for other reasons prisoners who warrant the trust can be given some freedom in the facility and be put to minor but productive tasks. Classification of prisoners as "trusties" or available for light work must be carefully done to avoid escapes and other problems.

All security measures must be established on a basis that allows prompt implementation of plans for evacuation of prisoners in the event of fire or facility destruction by other means. Planning must also provide full means of protection against the consequences of riot and mob attempts at rescue or attack. This may require provisions to quickly and inconspicuously move key prisoners to other detention.

Detention When Jails Unavailable

Most shelters and relocation facilities are not designed for detention purposes. This will require imaginative improvisation of both quarters and procedures. Two things must be provided in spite of adverse circumstances: (1) Basic security for prisoners, officers, and other occupants; and (2) separation of various categories of prisoners.

Large rooms, of course, can be used for group detention if adequate security is provided and if the need for separation is minimal or absent. Such use of space, however, may require the use of additional guards constantly on the alert to avoid altercations or plotting for escape.

In shelters the problems of security and separation may require unusual use of restraining devices and materials. Individual prisoners can be handcuffed to pipes, doorknobs, stanchions, or window bars. If this is done, adequate free space around the prisoner should be provided to avoid improper and dangerous contact with other prisoners or occupants of the shelter. Two prisoners can be secured with a single set of handcuffs merely by passing the cuffs behind a pipe set close to a wall or the floor, or behind a bar in a barred window or door.

Ropes, belts, and similar material may be used in lieu of handcuffs, but require unusual care to avoid injury or escapes. Although it may be necessary to occasionally check handcuffs to see that they are not too tight for the comfort or safety of the prisoner, frequent inspection of rope and other nonmetallic material is essential. These may quickly become either too tight and thus cause injury, or too loose and thus permit escape. Restraints of material must also be checked if they become wet, or dry out after being wet.

Sedatives may be used under unusual circumstances by a doctor or by a nurse under his direction. Sedatives have a particular value when handling a violent person and may be used both as a restraint and treatment in many cases.

Expensive, but necessary on occasion, will be the use of guards or officers on the basis of one guard to a prisoner. This should be avoided if possible because of the excessive drain it puts on available personnel.

Conclusion

It should be said once again that security is the essence of detention. The safety of officers, prisoners, and others is dependent on strict adherence to carefully prepared procedures.

CLASSIFICATION OF JAIL PRISONERS

TABLE OF CONTENTS

CLASSIFICATION OF JAIL PRISONERS

THE JAILER'S NEEDS TO KNOW

The days have gone forever when jails, other than those in large metropolitan areas, dealt almost exclusively with local citizens. Not only were the reputations and backgrounds of these people generally known, but commitment to jail was a conspicuous event. From his own knowledge and information readily available to him, the jailer could quickly size up the situation and determine how best to handle each prisoner. In these days of rapid community growth and mobility, when it is commonplace for people to relocate frequently and travel from one end of the country to the other in a few hours, increasing numbers of jail prisoners are commited as total strangers. Moreover, these people may have no ties whatever to the community in which the jail is located. The proper handling of prisoners who are strangers is an entirely different problem than dealing with people who are well known.

Within the limits of the law and the framework of judicial and public expectations, the chief jailer and his staff have wide latitude for making institutional policy decisions, establishing or changing operating procedures and introducing new methods, programs and services. While the exercise of this responsibility is in the interest of increasing the efficiency and effectiveness of basic jail functions, the inescapable fact is that jail personnel deal with people. For this reason, the manner in which policies, rules and procedures are applied have great importance. In part, this becomes a matter of sensitizing personnel to prisoners' needs, problems and feelings. In part, also, it is a matter of having information about individual prisoners with which to distinguish among them and to make decision choices based on these distinctions.

Just a brief look at a few ordinary jail activities will indicate how acute the need for information about prisoners can be. Take housing, for example. Any policy of housing jail prisoners will have to be determined to some extent by the kind and location of available accommodations. Yet, when choices are possible, common sense will dictate that: juvenile and female prisoners are held in seperate quarters; weak and submissive prisoners are not placed in dormitories or group cells with aggressive predatory types; prisoners with incapacitating physical handicaps are assigned to quarters on the main floor; young impressionable prisoners are separated from those who are sophisticated and calloused. Further reflection will suggest other distinctions.

2

One of the surest ways of inviting a law-suit, official or public censure and adverse prisoner reaction is to ignore or be unaware of a prisoner's need for emergency medical care. Will commitment policies permit the receiving officer to refuse acceptance of a person in need of immediate medical attention? If so, how does he discover that a problem exists and in what ways does he exercise this discretion? With whom and in what ways can prisoners register complaints of being ill? What is done about such complaints? What other kinds of emergency needs might arise which, if ignored, might cause great personal or family hardship or extreme and unnecessary inconvenience?

What is the work assignment policy at the jail? What should it be? How are trusties selected? Work release candidates? Many factors besides security have to be considered in making work assignment decisions. Is the prisoner physically able to the work required? A person with a heart condition, for example, or one subject to seizures should not be assigned to work in high places or at tasks requiring extreme physical exertion. Does the prisoner have the intelligence and emotional stability to follow instructions? Does he have the skills or experience that may be required? Will he take care of tools and equipment? Can he work cooperatively with others?

Adequate feeding can present problems. There may be dietary considerations, as for those who are under special medical care or those who live under strict religious observances. Food handlers should meet at least minimum public health standards of being free from infectious disease and neat in personal cleanliness. If there is a central dining room, it may be necessary to feed certain prisoners separately from certain others, such as a material witness who is to testify against a prisoner awaiting trial. When meals are served in housing units, there is a need to assure that the food is properly conveyed and that rations are distributed equitably. In this connection, it must be remembered that in group cells or dormitories weak inmates can be victimized by aggressive prisoners who will get more than their share.

Whatever correctional programs and services may be available obviously are intended for those prisoners who need them and who are eligible to participate in them. Increasing attention is being given such non-traditional pretrial programs as early diversion, pretrial liberty and emergency services to defendants and such post-conviction procedures as extending the limits of confinement. These suggest a number of possible new roles for jails for which new capabilities and more information about prisoners will be needed.

So the jailer has various needs for various kinds of information about prisoners; and these can be defined in fairly specific terms. One kind of information is that which has *predictive value*. Information of this kind is essential to good decision-making. To illustrate: it must be decided whether to place a prisoner under maximum or minimum supervision. The prisoner's stability is an important factor in such a decision. Residence is one indicator of stability, but how long he has been a resident of the community probably is more relevant than other kinds of information about residence. Thus, in this illustration, length of residence has predictive value in determining a person's stability, whereas the address or amount of rent does not.

Another kind of information is that which can be used for *identification purposes*. Essential distinctions are made among prisoners constantly. Is he in jail awaiting trial or serving a sentence? It makes a difference. It also matters whether he will be in jail a few days or several months. Identifying information is indispensible to good decision-making. It would make little sense, for example, to enroll in Alcoholics Anonymous a prisoner who did not at least have a serious drinking problem.

A third kind of information is that which is needed for *management evaluations*. Budget requests are sought and defended in such terms as daily per capita costs for care, custody and various kinds of programs and services. Changes in policy and other management adjustments are made in part on evaluations of day-to-day operations and activities. Planning for future requirements cannot proceed very far without factual accounts of the present and careful analyses of trends. These are but a few examples of many needs for information about prisoners, their circumstances, their management and control.

5

THE DEVELOPMENT AND TESTING OF A CLASSIFICATION TOOL

The focus of concern in this project is the jailer's decision-making responsibility and whether certain kinds of information about prisoners can be obtained and used in ways which will contribute to more prompt and reliable decisions. The jailer makes many decisions of many kinds. This project is limited primarily to determinations of prisoner custody (supervision requirements) and housing assignments. These are important basic decisions that are made tens of thousands of times every day in jails throughout the United States.

This is not a new concern. For a long time jailers have rightly complained of the extreme difficulties imposed upon them in exercising their responsibilities for the safekeeping of all kinds of prisoners who come and go daily. Underlying the burden is the absence of essential information with which to make important decisions based on factual experience and differences in prisoners. Past attempts have been made to adapt to the jail setting diagnostic and case management techniques of major prisons and reformatories. These efforts have been quite unproductive for reasons which are increasingly apparent. Informational needs have not been pin-pointed. Although both prisons and jails are lock-ups, the operation of a local jail is very much unlike that of a prison for sentenced felons. Most jails have neither the staff specialists nor the time to apply diagnostic procedures that are suitable for prisons.

Development of this experimental classification tool has been predictated on certain beliefs or assumptions. (1) It is possible to pin-point the jailers information needs and to distinguish various kinds of information in accordance with the uses for it. (2) From an array of information it is possible to select specific items which will have identification and predictive value for decision-making. (3) The kinds of information needed for basic decisions related to the management and control of jail prisoners can be obtained promptly and easily. (4) Information uses can be simplified and standardized.

DESIGN OF AN EXPERIMENTAL PROCEDURE

From years of experience in classifying sentenced prisoners and from published designs of bail reform procedures, items of information were listed which were thought to have a significant bearing on decisions as to prisoner supervision and housing assignments. More specifically, the object was to find what were thought to be the best indicators of emotional stability and mature behavior habits. The list was revised many times to insure that it included only the kinds of information that could be obtained during a brief interview, subject to quick and simple verification as might be necessary. The list was reduced to what was thought to be only key items and it was arranged so that it could be recorded by simply checking "yes" or "no" responses to direct questions.

The next task was to isolate the stability indicators and assign reasonable numerical weights to them since it could be expected that some items would be better predictors than others. It was also thought that some variables would be predictors only when measured in combination with other variables. Classification experience also suggested that not every important information item lends itself to variable weighting. Some items produce simple "either"-"or" decisions. It was known only that, by whatever means, the predictive values of the information at hand would have to be substantially greater than chance or the information would be useless as a decision-making aid.

With these considerations in mind, the information list was amended further and converted into an inventory of basic prisoner data which contained a mix of both predictive variables and items of identification that presumably would be helpful in decision-making, plus a few other items that might be useful for other purposes. Two overlay sheets were designed: one intended as an aid in determining degree of supervision required; the other as an aid to making housing assignments. Both were adapted to a prisoner inventory form with window cut-outs matched to the possible responses to certain information questions. The supervision overlay was geared to three grades of custody (maximum, medium and minimum supervision) in contrast to the usual two (trusties and all others) and included both "either"-"or" and weighted variable items of information. The housing overlay was limited to "either"-"or" items of information with a coded explanation of how these should be considered in making housing assignments.

The prisoner inventory and the two overlays were subjected to two pretests. The first was against the case records of 50 randomly selected Federal prisoners. This group was not like a random group of jail prisoners in that they were all adult males serving sentences, but they had been classified as to custody and housing. Inventory sheets were completed from information contained in the case records. Both overlay sheets were applied. The housing overlay showed nothing significant but the custody overlay produced a spread of maximum, medium and minimum custody decision recommendations that conformed roughly with decisions that had already been made.

Adjustments were made in some of the inventory items and in the scoring weights of the custody overlay. These manipulations produced greater conformity with the 50 case records of decisions already made. These revisions were further pretested with nearby jail prisoners A set of 109 additional inventories were completed from actual interviews. The revised custody overlay produced tabulated results that showed a nearly normal distribution of maximum, medium and minimum custody candidates. Unfortunately, there was no way of comparing these findings with actual custody decisions since neither of the cooperating jails had such a classification system. Likewise, because of the nature of both facilities, there was no way of utilizing the housing assignment overlay.

PRELIMINARY TESTS

With this encouragement, it was decided that the materials should be put to experimental use. The items of information for decision-making were rearranged again to further simplify their recording and use. A few new items were added, not for decision-making but to demonstrate the convenience and usefulness of a single record of basic information that could serve many administrative and management purposes. It was also thought that the numerically weighted values of certain information items used for custody decisions could also be used to predict certain kinds of actual behavior. In other words, it was assumed that the higher the numerical score the more likely the prisoner would be to accept the circumstances of his imprisonment and to relate satisfactorily to fellow prisoners and staff members. Accordingly, a questionnaire was added to the back of the prisoner inventory to test this assumption.

Following is the experimental Prisoner Inventory as it was prepared for use during a predetermined 60 day test period at selected jails. Both overlays were readied by final editing to insure that self-contained instructions were as complete and clear as possible. To these was added a set of general instructions for the actual use tests.

9

Prisoner Inventory Test

INSTRUCTIONS FOR PRISONER INVENTORY

It is intended that the Prisoner Inventory be completed for each prisoner admitted to jail, on the basis of a brief interview and such additional verifications as may be necessary. This may be done as part of the booking process. If not done then, the Inventory should be completed as soon after booking as possible. NOTE: The Prisoner Inventory is designed to be used only for healthy male prisoners. Females and prisoners who obviously are in need of immediate medical care should be considered special cases.

The upper part of the Prisoner Inventory consists of information items that have a bearing on decisions as to housing and supervision required. Overlay sheets, which carry their own instructions, are provided to assist in making these two decisions. The information contained in this portion of the Inventory, along with that appearing on the lower part, may have other possible uses as well. Check the YES or NO column for each category of items. Most check marks will appear in the YES column, but check only the one that is appropriate. Example, in the category of "AGE", the prisoner is either legally a juvenile, under 21, between 21 and 25, between 26 and 35 or over 35. Check one.

As a guide to deciding the degree of custody or amount of supervision required for the prisoner, *carefully* place the Supervision overlay sheet on top of the completed Prisoner Inventory so that the proper items show through the windows. Look first for W items that show through, then add the numerical values of all the other items that show. Enter W or the total score on the top of the Inventory sheet. Consult the instructions on the overlay sheet as a guide to custody decision. There is reason to believe that this indication is reliable, ***but it is not a substitute for common sense.***

For housing decisions follow the same procedure of matching the overlay sheet to the Inventory form. The numbers at the windows, however, are not to be added. They are code numbers that are keyed to specific instructions on the bottom of the overlay sheet. Note that these are not substitutes for common sense.

To assist in the experimental use of these forms, enter the custody classification and housing assignment at the upper left hand corner of the Prisoner Inventory form. Whenever either of these classifications may be changed, enter the date and the change on the top of the form, from left to right, so that the last entry on the right will be the current one.

There is a question as to whether the decision-maker should be the same person who completed the Prisoner Inventory. For experimental purposes this does not matter. If the same employee performs both functions he may develop certain biases that will cause him to complete the Inventory to coincide with what he thinks the outcome should be. It is possible, too, that in some jails decisions of this kind are made only by supervisory personnel. On the other hand, a rating instrument of any kind can never be all-inclusive or perfect. This one is not a substitute either for common sense or for knowledge, experience and skills in dealing with people. From this point of view, it is possible that the person completing the Inventory can make better decisions because his personal contact with the prisoner is better than relying entirely on a piece of paper that somebody else provided.

Again, because of great differences in the nature of jail operations, it may not be necessary to complete the Prisoner Inventory form on all persons booked. For example, the value of completed forms for offenders who will be held in jail for only a few hours or a day or two may be questioned.

On the back of the Prisoner Inventory form is a questionnaire relative to prisoner characteristics and behavior that were observed. This should be completed as part of the experiment by the jail supervisor or other staff member who is in a posistion to know. The evaluation should be made on the day of the prisoner's release from jail or at the end of the 60-day experiment, whichever comes first. Simply place a check mark in the appropriate column as to each item, record any additional comments; enter date, signature and title.

All Prisoner Inventory forms must be picked up by the Jail Inspector at the conclusion of the 60-day trial period and mailed promptly to the Bureau. Review and analysis of the data will be primarily for the purpose of determining the reliability of the forms as a decision-making guide. In addition, it is hoped that the forms will be an aid in predicting the behavior of certain catagories of prisoners.

DEGREE OF SUPERVISION REQUIRED*

PRISONER INVENTORY

	RATING	YES	NO
COMMITMENT STATUS			
On writ	W		
Other	W		
Possible detainers	W		
Prior commitment	3		
AGE			
Juvenile	W		
21-25	1		
26-35	2		
Over 35	3		
MARITAL STATUS			
Married	3		
Family support —			
total	3		
major	2		
partial	1		

	RATING	YES	NO
RESIDENCE			
Duration— ** (see footnote)			
under 6 mos.	1-0		
6 mos. to 1 yr.	2-1		
over 1 yr.	3-2		
Duration in community —			
under 6 mos.	1-0		
6 mos. to 1 yr.	2-1		
over 1 yr.	3-2		
Rents by —			
month	2		
Leasing or pur.	3		
Lives with family	3		
RECENT WORK HISTORY			
Employed or in school —			
full time	3		
part time	2		
under 6 mos.	1		
6 mos. to 1 yr.	2		
over 1 yr.	3		

	RATING	YES	NO
MENTAL CONDITION OR ATTITUDE			
Appears or acts —			
questionable	W		
abnormal	W		

* to be used for healthy male prisoners only—females, and prisoners in need of medical care, are to be considered special cases.

**if residence is in local community, use left hand rating figures; if not, use right hand rating figures.

NOTES

Purpose: Only those items of the Prisoner Inventory thought to have a direct bearing on custody decisions are used.

Rating legend: 3 denotes a good indicator of stability.
2 denotes a fair indicator of stability.
1 denotes a minimum indicator of stability.
W (Warning) is an indicator of probable instability.
(Any W item checked means that in the absence of any compeling reason to the contrary, the prisoner should not be placed in reduced custody and may require maximum supervision at all times.)

Scoring: W: If a check mark appears for any item rated W, the prisoner should be classified maximum custody until further investigation or a change of circumstances suggests otherwise.

10 or less	: a good candidate for maximum custody.
11 - 15	: a questionable candidate for medium custody.
16 - 20	: a good candidate for medium custody.
21 - 25	: a questionable candidate for minimum custody.
26 - 30	: a good candidate for minimum custody.

522-838 O - 73 - 2

13

PRISONER INVENTORY

NAME: NUMBER: DATE: TIME:

	YES	NO		YES	NO		YES	NO
COMMITMENT STATUS			ESTIMATED STAY			MENTAL CONDITION		
Awaiting trial			One day or less			OR ATTITUDE		
Awaiting sentence			2 days to 1 wk.			Appears or acts —		
Awaiting appeal			Over 1 wk. to 1 mo.			normal		
Direct sentence or fine			Over 1 mo. to 6 mos.			questionable		
Parole violation			Over 6 mos. to 1 yr.			abnormal		
On writ			Over 1 yr.			describe:		
Other			RESIDENCE					
specify:			Address:					
			Duration —					
			under 6 mos.					
Possible detainers			6 mos. to 1 yr.					
explain:			over 1 yr.			PHYSICAL CONDITION		
			Duration in community —			General appearance —		
			under 6 mos.			good		
			6 mos. to 1 yr.			questionable		
			over 1 yr.			poor		
Prior commitment			Rents by —			Present complaint		
AGE			day or week			explain:		
Juvenile			month					
Under 21			Leasing or purchasing					
21-25			Lives with family					
26-35			RECENT WORK HISTORY					
Over 35			Employer's name			Taking medication		
SEX			and address:			description:		
Male								
Female								
CHARGE OR OFFENSE								
Against person			Employed or in school —					
Sex			full time			Doctor's care		
Property			part time			physician's name:		
Public order			odd jobs					
Other			unemployed					
MARITAL STATUS			under 6 mos.					
Married			6 mos. to 1 yr.					
Family support —			over 1 yr.					
total			WORK SKILLS (describe)			Appearance or		
major						history of —		
partial						alcohol		
none						drugs		

Describe prisoner's responsibilities, if any:

Persons interested in this prisoner:

Name	Address	Tel.	Relation

Immediate problems: (list in order of importance) (Action indicated)

Other observations or comments:

14

Prisoner Characteristics and Behavior	True	More True Than False	More False Than True	Un-true	Don't Know
General Adjustment					
1. Accepted circumstances without complaints.					
2. Behavior was satisfactory and dependable.					
3. Participated in available activities regularly.					
4. Positive outlook toward release.					
5. Escaped or attempted escape.					
Relationships with Personnel					
1. Cooperative and respectful.					
2. Accepted instructions and constructive criticism.					
3. Sought no personal favors; did not fraternize.					
4. Enjoyed the confidence and respect of personnel.					
Relationships with Prisoners					
1. Sought few associates and chose them carefully.					
2. Respectful and considerate.					
3. Self-assured; maintained own identity.					
4. Enjoyed the confidence and respect of others.					

Comments:

Date:	Signature:	Title:

HOUSING*

PRISONER INVENTORY

	CODE NO.	YES	NO
COMMITMENT STATUS			
Awaiting trial	1		
Awaiting sentence	1		
Other	2		
Prior commitment	3		
AGE			
Juvenile	4		
Under 21	5		
SEX			
Female	6		
CHARGE OR OFFENSE			
Against person	7		
Sex	8		

	CODE NO.	YES	NO
MENTAL CONDITION OR ATTITUDE			
Appears or acts —			
questionable	9		
abnormal	9		
PHYSICAL CONDITION			
General appearance —			
questionable	9		
poor	9		
Doctor's care	9		
Appearance or history of —			
alcohol	9		
drugs	9		

*to be used for all commitments

Code No	Action
1	Should be kept apart from sentenced prisoners if possible.
2	Should be kept apart from sentenced prisoners if possible and if material witness, awaiting sanity hearing, etc., may require separate quarters.
3	The degree of supervision required and the conduct record of a prior commitment are good in-ricators of what can be expected on this commitment.
4	Must be kept entirely separate from all adults.
5	If weak submissive type, may need protection from sophisticated, aggressive types.
6	Must be kept entirely separate from all males.
7	Others may need protection from aggressive, predatory types.
8	Child molesters and rapists may need protection from others. Aggressive homosexuals may need to be segregated, passive homosexuals may need protection.
9	Obtain medical advice for housing requirements.

For an adequate test it was hoped that five or six jails could be selected that would represent geographical spread, different size and various kinds of operations. It was also hoped that local jail officials could be found who would be willing and able to make operational changes during the 60-day test period in order that decisions called for by the classification forms could actually be applied. Six such jails were identified and the Federal Jail Inspectors responsible for them were brought together for briefings on the test and discussions of the kinds of operational changes that might be considered. They were also informed how to help jail personnel prepare for the test experience. The kinds of assistance that might be needed to complete the experiment were anticipated. It was determined that the test period should run from May 1 to June 30, 1970. As soon as the test ended the Inspectors involved were to collect all of the completed forms and send them to the private consulting agency in New York City with whom a contract was made for processing and analyzing the test data. (See Appendix B for the summary report).

Major test findings: A single general conclusion about the experiment, such as that it succeeded or failed, would have little meaning. The fact is that in both operational and analytical terms the test experience was highly encouraging in a number of particulars and just as disappointing in others. The experiment also produced some outcomes that were unforeseen.

Findings related to basic assumptions. Assumption (1): It is possible to pin-point the jailers information needs and to distinguish various kinds of information in accordance with the uses for it. The test confirmed this. All information items used in the test were specific and they were of three distinct types, all of which were applied in one way or another. Assumption (2): From an array of information it is possible to select specific items which will have identification and predictive value for decision-making. The test confirmed this. See discussion of findings related to experimental assumptions, below, and Appendix B. Assumption (3): The kinds of information needed for basic decisions can be obtained promptly and easily. The test confirmed this. Interviews with new prisoners were conducted at the time of booking or soon thereafter. Interviews were completed in ten minutes or less each by line officers who were given minimum instructions in how to conduct such interviews. Decisions as to custody and housing assignments were made instantly. Assumption (4): Information uses can be simplified and standardized. The test confirmed this. See the custody and housing overlays both of which were used simultaneously in six different jails for a period of 60 days.

Findings related to experimental assumptions. Assumption (a): It is possible to classify jail prisoners into three grades of custody, instead of the usual two. The test confimed this. Of 1,735 prisoners processed in six jails over a 60-day period 743 were classified maximum custody, 886 medium custody and 106 minimum custody. Assumption (b): An instrument can be designed which will reliably identify which prisoners should be classified maximum, medium and minimum custody. The test provided statistical encouragement that this is possible. See Appendix B. There was about a .70 level of correlation between recommended custody and actual custody decisions in all test jails. Assumption (c): An instrument can be designed which will help to avoid improper and unwise housing assignments. The test provided neither positive nor negative clues as to this. Whether because of lack of understanding or reluctance to modify operational customs for a limited test period, there was little indication that available housing accommodations were differentiated or stratified to enable a test of this assumption. Assumption (d): The scoring values used in making custody decisions can also be used to predict prisoner behavior. The test provided neither positive nor negative clues as to this. No answers were recorded on this part of the Prisoner Inventory forms in over three-fourths of them. With many entries incomplete on the remaining one-forth, meaningful data analysis was impossible.

While these results are directly related to the primary purposes of the test, the experiment produced a number of other significant findings:

The Prisoner Inventory itself can be a useful identifier of prisoner types. Examples: Officials at one jail expressed surprise at finding so high a proportion of drug users. At another jail staff expressed surprise at the number of young prisoners awaiting trial on serious charges. At a third jail the Prisoner Inventory documented the burdensome process of repeated bookings of habitual drunks.

The Prisoner Inventory can provide information that is useful in identifying correctional needs of prisoners. The jail with the high proportion of drug users planned to seek the assistance of the county medical association in treating this problem. The same jail began to think about ways of increasing prisoners' educational achievement.

In the four test jails where breakdowns of one kind or another did not force abandonment of the experiment, jail officials were unanimous in their observation that the project contributed to a marked improvement in prisoner attitudes and staff morale. The possibility of this kind of benefit had not been foreseen in the experimental design and in the absence of scientific measures of what actually happened one can only speculate about it. Perhaps the prisoners who were interviewed reacted in positive ways to the attention they received (and possibly to the implicit expectation that the interviews were conducted for some beneficial purpose). It is possible that personnel found reassurance in a better understanding of prisoners as people with the new information produced. It could be that the face-to-face relationship which an interview requires has its own training value for staff. This is to say that as staff begins to look upon prisoners in new and different ways, this triggers new thoughts and ideas about prisoners and about the job of managing them in jail.

The test produced another important finding: this or any other approach to the classification of jail prisoners will fail without (a) real commitment to it by administrators and supervisors; (b) adequate staff training and operational preparation and (c) supervision to insure consistency in application. These lessons can be clearly seen in Appendix A which briefly describes each of the test jails and summarizes each of the test experiences. Despite the best of pretest intentions to minimize breakdowns and misunderstandings, the facts are that two jails abandoned the project after the first week or two, none completed all of the Prisoner Inventory forms and none fully applied the kinds of decisions that the project was supposed to test. This is not stated as an indictment at all and any blame for this disappointing performance must be shared by the project directors and the Jail Inspectors involved. This finding is invaluable as an aid to any further experimentation.

FUTURE POSSIBILITIES

Although the experiment was incomplete in a number of respects it has demonstrated some of its potentials of one approach to the classification of jail prisoners. Preliminary experience with this approach suggests that it can be useful to jail managers in a number of ways and that it can be applied with relative safety.

That the basic Prisoner Inventory and the overlays need further refinement is beyond question. While, as a whole, the Prisoner Inventory form produced very few "no answers" during the test some items were responded to more completely than others. Further adjustments are needed to reduce "no answers" to absolute minimums. Through application in other jail settings and further analysis it should be possible to increase the sensitivity and reliability of the system as a decision-making aid. The underlying concept, and the forms used can be developed to meet other jail management needs. For example, information can be gathered and recorded to create an essential prisoner information system. Information can be used to identify and assess the nature of prisoners' correctional needs. Further experimentation may enable the development of classification materials as diagnostic and predictive instruments for the use of correctional program managers, judges and other concerned officials both within and outside the criminal justice system.

An effective prisoner classification system can have even more immediate operational benefits. (1) Improved security and control of prisoners will be assured through identifying and providing necessary surveillance for those who need closest supervision. Direct benefits should be realized in fewer escapes, assaults, destruction of property and similar behavior which is disruptive and threatening to good order and safety. (2) It should be possible for administrators and supervisors to use available personnel more efficiently. When prisoner housing assignments, work assigments and other activities are stratified and regulated according to custody classifications, supervision and controls are applied where needed and only to the extent circumstances require. (3) The combination of (1) and (2) should result in greater flexibility in jail operations. For example, minimum custody prisoners can be permitted more activity than others. Minimum custody housing units can be of less secure construction, more remotely located and checked less frequently than others. Personnel deployment can be concentrated or diluted in accordance with custody groups of prisoners, as well as the supervision requirements of various activities and the time of day. (4) When privileges and opportunities to participate in various activities are geared to custody classifications there will be built-in incentive for most prisoners to aspire to the most favorable grades of custody. This implies that prisoners can and will be reclassified upward or downward as their attitudes, behavior and circumstances warrant. (5) An effective system of prisoner classification will provide a data base for periodic reexamination of policy, evaluations of operating efficiency and future planning. This is to say that factual information about prisoner characteristics, their needs for control and services and the manner of their adaptation to confinement can be translated into requirements of correctional program planning and architectural design of new facilities.

Hopefully, this project has suggested a degree of confidence is warranted that a system for classifying jail prisoners can be engineered and applied. There can be no question that the pay-offs of such a system will be worth the effort and expense. May the project have provided the inspiration for further explorations.

Appendix A

JAIL A is a small, rural type jail in the Southwest built in 1919 with a total capacity of 74. Many of the prisoners are local Indians serving short sentences on drunkenness charges. Housing is of inside cell type with a day room. All maintenance work is performed by 8 trusties. Activities are limited to religious services conducted by lay preachers, day room recreation, use of donated reading materials and personal radios.

A few of the Prisoner Inventory forms were completed but no attempt was made to use the information for decision-making and the statisticians were unable to process the data. The Jail Sergeant felt that the forms did help discover a possible T.B. case and identify a number of prisoners who were supposed to be on some type of medication. For the most part, he felt, the Inventory was of no value. In his words, "It sure don't work on Indians."

JAIL B is a fairly new metropolitan jail in the Southeast with a rated capacity of 955. Two other separate units are operated conjointly with it; a new lock-up for traffic offenders and a minimum security stockade, primarily for sentenced prisoners. At the main jail there are several types of single and group cell housing. All work except food service is performed by stockade trusties. Other activities include worship services and religious education classes, individual and group counseling, central radio, TV and dayroom recreation.

This jail was, by far, the largest contributor to the test sample. Nearly 1,200 prisoners were processed during the two-month period. Unfortunately, entries were not made on the back of the Prisoner Inventory form. Thus it was not possible to analyze the relationship between supervision scores and subsequently observed behavior and characteristics. During the test period all newly-commited prisoners were kept in holding cells until they were classified. The test material was used in limited ways for housing assignments, selection of trusties and seperation of medical cases needing special attention. Jail officials expressed surprise at finding so high a proportion of young offenders and unmarried drug users. It was thought that more minimum custody candidates should have been identified by the classification material and staff began to see the need for additional information on the Prisoner Inventory form, such as drug use and educational achievement.

Staff consensus was that test materials were highly useful. It was observed that prisoners were more at ease and more cooperative than formerly. This was attributed to the personal attention given during classification interviews. Staff planned to seek County Medical Association help for the drug users and educational and guidance opportunities for the younger offenders. Officials planned to continue the project after the test period ended and to use the experience as a basis for developing their own classification system.

JAIL C is another new city jail and is located on the Gulf Coast. It has a normal capcity of 487 and operates as a detention center primarily for adult males awaiting trial and sentenced prisoners on appeal. All booking occurs at a separate 166-man unit downtown. The main jail has a unit of maximum security single cells, a minimum custody wing and units of 4-man group cells. Unit day rooms are provided. Sentenced prisoners work on the farm and perform maintenance chores. Other activities include chapel services for minimum custody prisoners, dayroom recreation and donated reading material.

Staff used the classification material to a limited extent in making both housing and work assignments. Staff expressed surprise at the number of young prisoners awaiting trial on serious charges. They felt that the Prisoner Inventory form enabled the identification of medical problems that otherwise might have been missed. The form was used to check identity of visitors. The "who-to-notify" item was used several times. Staff experimented in using the classification material to identify additional prisoners who would be allowed to attend Chapel services. This ended when a "grand fight" resulted from unknown enemies getting together. Despite this, it was felt that the classification interviews enabled staff to know the prisoners better and that this tended to ease prisoner stress. It was also felt that Inventory information would be useful in planning a new jail by enabling design to meet the needs of more specific prisoner types.

JAIL D too, is a new jail located in a North Central city. With a normal capacity of 256, housing accomodations consist of 12-bed dormitories and inside single cells. An attempt is made to employ all sentenced prisoners. In addition to performing maintenance chores around the jail, trusties perform such work in town as doing the janitor work at the court house. Other activities include remedial education, group therapy, Alcoholics Anonymous, psychological testing, vocational training in auto mechanics and welding and reading materials furnished by the State Library.

Classification interviews were conducted by two identification officers immediately after booking. The information was used in making work assignments for sentenced prisoners, but many prisoners were well known to staff and this knowledge tended to override decisions indicated by the classification rating sheet. Housing unit officers completed the back of the Prisoner Inventory form as required. Staff discovered that a large proportion of prisoners booked were actually held only a few hours or a day or two. The Inventory forms also documented the burdensome process of repeated bookings of habitual drunks. The Sheriff intended to use these facts to support an attempt to find ways of circumventing customary jail routines for these offenders. The Sheriff also thought that morale of both prisoners and staff improved during the test period. This was attributed to positive prisoner reaction to the attention given them and a corresponding tendency of staff to relax. Staff thought that the classification project would be even more valuable in a large metropolitan jail where most of the prisoners are unknown.

JAIL E is located in a South Central city. With a normal capacity of 364, this jail was built in 1925 but it was renovated and remodeled twice in the 1960's. Housing consists of single cells with front day rooms. This unit operates in conjunction with another 150-man holding facility for lesser offenders and the County Penal Farm. The Farm is intended for all sentenced prisoners as well as persons who will await trial for any length of time. As a result, activities at the main jail are rather limited. Only a few prisoners are assigned to maintenance chores. There is day room recreation, central radio, worship services and reading material furnished by local church and civic groups.

At the outset of the test period, arrangements had been made for one staff member to do all the classification interviewing but he became ill and the interviewing was relegated to housing unit officers on each of 3 floors whose work shifts changed every 4 weeks. This unfortunate circumstance interfered with proper completion of the Prisoner Inventory forms and with experimental decision-making. Despite this, there was staff consensus that the experimental rating sheets tended to confirm "seat of the pants" impressions of prisoners. Staff expressed surprise at the large number of persons who were released on bond after booking and expressed the general view that classification interviews tended to relieve prisoner anxiety. On the basis of this fragmentary experience the Sheriff intends to improve the prisoner records system to reflect more information about each prisoner and to develop their own classification program.

JAIL F is a city jail on the Mexican border. It has a normal capacity of 448. Housing consists of both inside single and group cells, in addition to which there are dormitories for trusties. Sentenced misdemeanants perform necessary maintenance chores around the jail and they are housed separately. At the time of the test there were few other activities but plans had been completed for a demonstration grant to finance a group of correctional programs clustered around vocational training and work release.

Rather elaborate plans were made for the experimental classification project to insure that both housing and work assignments were based on the test materials. Tentative arrangements were also made for follow-up counseling and referral of prisoner problems to local agencies. All new prisoners were to be kept in holding cells until they were classified. Interviewing was to be done by booking officers under the supervision of a counselor who was to have functioned in effect as project director. Everything went as planned for the first two weeks but then the counselor left, several English-speaking jailers went on vacation and there was not sufficient help left to conduct interviews and do the paper work. A week after the experiment was prematurely terminated one prisoner murdered another. There was some speculation that this might have been avoided had the original classification plan been in effect. By the end of the test period some stratification of housing was left but there was no formal means of classifying prisoners.

Appendix B

PRISONER INVENTORY STUDY

October, 1970

OBJECTIVES

The purpose of the present study was to evaluate the effectiveness of two scoring systems currently being developed to help estimate required supervision for prisoners and housing requirements. The two scoring systems were:

1) the Estimated Supervision Score based on answers to the Prisoner Inventory — a series of questions about the prisoners commitment status, background and appearance.

2) the Prisoners Characteristics Score, based on answers to questions about prisoners adjustment and relationships to personnel and other prisoners.

Each of these two estimated scores were constructed based on responses from a sample of jails, and *validated* against an *actual* supervision code assigned by wardens using normal procedures.

In addition, the present study offered an opportunity to evaluate other aspects of the effectiveness of the scoring systems such as *ease of response*, *sensitivity* of the scores and of the items making up the scores, and *reliability* of the scores across the various jails.

METHOD

1. Sample

   The sample size was 1,846. The surveys were taken in five jails: Dade County, East Baton Rouge County, Ingham County, El Paso County, and Shelby County.

2. Data Problems

   The following is a discussion of the problems which were incurred in the initial retrieval of the data from the forms.

   a. Dade County did not fill in the backs of the questionnaires.

   b. Dade County sent carbon copies which were not properly aligned.

   c. Instructions for filling out both the Estimated Supervision Code and the Housing Code were not followed at all.

   d. Housing Classification (single, group, dorm) was not coded.

e. Multiple responses were listed, in which case the first response was recorded.

f. The Charge or Offense category was often qualified and/or answered as "other". Possibly this category should be expanded.

3. <u>Definitions of Calculations</u>

a. Estimated Supervision Code was calculated according to specification.

b. Housing Code was calculated according to specification. If the person fell into two or more codes, each was counted.

c. The average scores for General Adjustment, Relations and Personnel, Relations with Prisoners and Prisoner Characteristics, were determined in the following manner:

1) Drop all "Don't know" answers.

2) Assign the following values:

a) true = 1

b) more false than true = 2

c) more true than false = 3

d) false = 4

3) Sum all values for each category.

4) Multiply the above sum by 10.

5) Divide the result in 4) by the number of "1-4" answers in each category.

The Prisoner Characteristics Average Score includes all categories.

CONCLUSION

1. IS THE ESTIMATED SUPERVISION SCORE BASED ON THE PRISONER INVENTORY AN EFFECTIVE SYSTEM FOR ESTIMATING DEGREE OF SUPERVISION REQUIRED?

Yes. The ESS was based on questions which elicited high levels of response from wardens. It appears to be a *sensitive* and *reliable* tool, most importantly, a *valid* means of estimating the actual supervision code for prisoners.

a. Response rates for ESS questions

As a whole, the ESS questions resulted in very few "no answers" indicating that the Prisoner Inventory questions are practical and easy to obtain answers for.

Some items, however, were less completely responded to than others, indicating possibilities for further refinement of questions to minimize "no answers" which adversely affects the ESS. (See Tables 29-50 for items in the Prisoner Inventory where "no answers" exceed 3% — e.g. family support, length of employment, etc.)

b. Sensitivity and Reliability of the ESS

The ESS appears to be a potentially sensitive tool. Scores from the sample for this study were distributed fairly equally across the whole scale, indicating a broad range of classifications which the ESS is capable of measuring. This dispersion of scores occurred in each of the five participating jails. (Table 1)

The ESS also appears to be a reliable tool: scores developed for each of the participating jails indicated a reasonably consistent dispersion of scores across all five jails. The ESS did as well as the Actual Supervision Codes on dispersion of the scores and consistency across jails. (Table 1, 2 through 7)

c. Validity of the ESS Relative to Actual Supervision Code.

The ESS appears to be a reasonably good estimate of the actual supervision code assigned by wardens under current practices. The ESS correlates well with both the "first" supervision code and the "last" supervision code — at about .70 level of correlation.

This holds true for the total sample of all jails and also for each of the individual jails as well. (Tables 81 to 86, 96 to 105).

2. DOES THE PRISONERS CHARACTERISTICS SCORE REPRESENT AN EFFECTIVE SYSTEM FOR ESTIMATING DEGREE OF SUPERVISION REQUIRED?

No. The questions on which this score was based were poorly responded to, both in number of responses and quality of response. Given the relatively poor raw data for this score, it is not surprising that the PCS did not prove to be a good predictor of the Actual Supervision Code. Nonetheless, there are some indications that the concept of the PCS as an estimating tool could work if improvements are made in the data obtained.

a. Response rates for the PCS questions

The bulk of the sample for this study, the 1176 residents (out of 1846) from Dade County, as well as about 300 respondents from the other cities, did not answer any of the questions on the Prisoners Characteristics and Behavior. Of those who *did* answer this section of the questionaire, many did not respond to all of the questions. (Tables 51-63)

b. Sensitivity and reliability of the PCS

In addition to the low response rates, the quality of responses to the PCS questions was very poor — many respondents checked the same answer for all items, not discriminating in their responses. As a result, the Prisoners Characteristics Score is not a potentially sensitive score. Most of the respondents fell into the most favorable category, indicating that the respondent gave a "True" answer to all 10 questions, excepting only the attempted "Escape" question.

Prisoner Characteristic Score	%
10 (Good)	54
11 to 19	35
20 + (Bad)	11
(See Tables 101 to 108)	100

There is also little consistency in the pattern of responses across the various jails — in one jail, as many as 85% are in the 10 score category, whereas in another jail, only 2% fell in the 10 score group, an indication of both a lack of reliability as well as a lack of sensitvity in the estimated score.
(Tables 109 — 140)

c. Validity of the PCS vs. Actual Supervision Code

As might be expected, given the poor data in the PCS, it does not correlate well with the actual supervision code (correlation of .23). Neither the total PCS, nor the components of the PCS — the average score on General Adjustment, or the average score on Relationships with Personnel, or the average score on Relationships with Prisoners — is a good estimate of the Actual Supervision Code. However, there is still an indication of a *slight* relationship even with the current PCS, when analyzed on a gross basis, suggesting that a PCS could work if the input data were better.

	Estimated PCS					
	Minimum (10 score)		Medium (11-19)		Maximum (20+)	
Actual First Supervision Code	#	%	#	%	#	%
Minimum	9	8	2	3	2	9
Medium	63	57	19	31	6	29
Maximum	38	35	40	66	13	62
	110	100	61	100	21	100

(See Tables 102, 104, 106, 108)

3. BASED ON THE PRESENT STUDY, WHAT ARE SOME WAYS IN WHICH THE TWO ESTIMATING TOOLS — THE ESS AND PCS — MIGHT BE IMPROVED?

The experience with the present study suggests that improvements could be made in the following aspects of these tools:

- improving response rates
- improving sensitivity of the scores by improving discrimination in responses to specific items.
- improving ease of handling data for analysis

a. Response rates — ESS and PCS

The ESS is reasonably effective as it now stands, and the only obvious area for improvement is to decrease no-answers by clarifying or amplifying some of the questions in the Prisoner Inventory.

The bigger problems lie with PCS. Presumably, response rates could be improved with clearer instructions to the respondents and stressing the importance of the questions on the back of the questionnaire.

b. Increasing sensitivity of PCS

In addition, however, changes should be made in the questions. The balanced 4 point scale currently used (True, More true than false, More false than true, False) for responses to the questions, resulted in answers clustering in either the first or second box; hardly anyone responded in the two "false" boxes. Thus, it would seem desirable to use either an unbalanced 4 point scale, (e.g. Completely true, Usually true, Sometimes true. Not true; where three boxes are positive, and only one is negative) or better yet, a 6 point or 10 point unbalanced scale. (e.g. Completely true, Very true, Quite true, Somewhat true, Not true, Not very true, Not at all true is a 6 point unbalanced scale — 4 positives and 2 negatives.)

c. Ease of handling data — ESS and PCS

Finally, greater ease in tabulating and handling the data could be accomplished by pre-coding the questionnaire for both ESS and PCS and by altering the layout somewhat. This might also serve a double purpose in making the questionnaire easier to answer for the respondents, thus increasing response rates as well.

4. Process

After the forms had been filled in, they were sent by each jail to the private consulting agency. Each form was then stamped with an identification number to identify the form and jail. The forms were then hand coded so that they could be keypunched. After the keypunching, they were edited to correct possible coding and keypunch errors. For this process the Data Check Express software package was used. Tabulation specifications were changed somewhat in view of the data. After seeing the results of the first set of tables, a second set was run to explore certain areas of the Supervision Codes.

www.ingramcontent.com/pod-product-compliance
Lightning Source LLC
Chambersburg PA
CBHW080324020526
44117CB00035B/2648
* 9 7 8 1 7 9 9 3 0 4 0 6 7 *